How to Start and Sustain a Faith-Based WOMEN'S SPIRITUALITY GROUP

How to Start and Sustain a Faith-Based

WOMEN'S SPIRITUALITY GROUP

Circle of Hearts

Patricia D. Brown

ABINGDON PRESS / NASHVILLE

HOW TO START AND SUSTAIN A FAITH-BASED
WOMEN'S SPIRITUALITY GROUP

Copyright © 2003 by Patricia D. Brown

This book is printed on acid-free paper.

Library of Congress Cataloging-in-Publication Data

Brown, Patricia D., 1953-
  How to start and sustain a faith-based women's spirituality group :
circle of hearts / Patricia D. Brown.
      p. cm.
  ISBN 0-687-04609-2 (bdg. : pbk. : alk. paper)
  1. Church work with women. 2. Christian women--Religious life. I.
Title.

BV4445 .B764 2003
259'.082--dc21

                                                         2002151116

"The Quest of the Woman in Search of Her Heart," is from *Heart to
Heart Guidebook* by Patricia Brown © 1999 Dimensions for Living.
Used by permission.

Some of the ideas in this book were first put forward in *Heart to Heart
Guidebook* by Patricia Brown © 1999 Dimensions for Living. Used by
permission.

Scripture quotations are from the *New Revised Standard Version Bible,*
copyright 1989, by the Division of Christian Education of the National
Council of the Churches of Christ in the United States of America. Used
by permission. All rights reserved.

        03 04 05 06 07 08 09 10 11 12 —10 9 8 7 6 5 4 3 2 1

                MANUFACTURED IN THE UNITED STATES OF AMERICA

CONTENTS

Acknowledgments 7

Introduction: Sister to Sister 9

1. The Busy Woman's Guide to Spirituality . . . 13

2. Core Characteristics of Women's Christian
   Spirituality Circles 34

3. Birthing Your Circle 49

4. Opening Moments to the Final Amen 76

5. Sacred Story Bible Study 92

6. Prayer Rituals 119

7. Be-Attitudes for Circles 135

8. Will the Circle Be Unbroken? 144

9. Resources for Your Circle 156

Benediction: Finding Our Path 166

ACKNOWLEDGMENTS

Only by letting ourselves be known to each other and to our deepest selves can we have the assurance that we are known by God.
— *Margaret Guenther,* Holy Listening

My circle of sisters grows larger and more expansive the farther I travel in life. I am grateful to all the women, past and present, who stand in the circle with me. I am aware of the large number who have taught me what it means to be in a blessed community. They have cared for my soul during periods of searching and writing, and even now they sustain me. "I thank my God every time I remember you, constantly praying with joy in every one of my prayers for all of you, because of your sharing in the gospel from the first day until now" (Philippians 1:3-5).

Thanks to my mom, Arlene Griffith Brown, for birthing a girl child (me), and to my delightful sister and new best friend, Barbara Brown Downs. Thanks also to my friend Adele Wilcox, who read every word of this manuscript and offered advice and encouragement. To my women colleagues of the

Central Pennsylvania Conference of The United Methodist Church and to all the women who sustain me with wit, wisdom, support, encouragement, and accountability—I am grateful.

I was blessed to have the inspired editorial guidance of Sally Sharpe, who helped all the pages and words hang together.

And finally, my gratitude to all the pioneering sisters through the centuries who have walked these paths before me. Like them, may we also find the courage to be a compass for those to come. And praise to the Spirit who leads us all.

INTRODUCTION:

Sister to Sister

I write books because I find they are some of the best spiritual teachers I have. In the past, I have been mysteriously drawn—sometimes kicking and screaming—to topics and issues with which I am personally struggling. This book is no exception. In the course of writing, I am forced to clarify many of my own thoughts and feelings. I must sort out my "her-story"—the good, the bad, and the ugly—face my failings, and celebrate my victories.

In writing this book, I have struggled with angels and demons. I have discovered within myself feelings about women's groups and spirituality that are deeper and more complex than I ever imagined. I've had a variety of experiences with women's Christian spirituality groups through the years—the vast majority good, a few not so hot. So it was with some trepidation that I set out on this journey. Women's Christian spirituality groups are "risky business";

anytime you are in the same room with a group of powerful women and the Holy Spirit, look out!

This confession, of sorts, isn't meant to scare you off. Indeed, my hope is that this book will help you begin a journey with other sisters of faith. As you start your own women's Christian spirituality group, remember that there are no rules—no right or wrong ways to do it. I guarantee the road will be full of surprises. My hopes and prayers are that you will find with your sisters a place that will sustain you in your tears, make you laugh, and heal you.

My purpose in writing this book is twofold: to share with you what I have learned about women's Christian spirituality groups and to help you begin your own group. In short, this book is about the theory and practice of being sisters and friends.

The book is divided into nine chapters. In the first two chapters, I lay out the theory and theology of the spirituality circle—but don't be put off by this description. You'll find these chapters to be full of biblically grounded, commonsense stuff. They will give you a deeper appreciation of the mysterious creative Spirit that will flourish in your circle. In chapters 3 and 4, I help you get your circle up and running by discussing the nuts and bolts of starting a group, from the first invitation to the final amen. Chapters 5 and 6 follow with step-by-step instructions for using techniques in Bible study and prayer ritual that will enrich your gathering. Then, to keep your circle healthy, look to chapters 7 and 8 for the "Be-Attitudes" of a Christ-centered group and matter-of-fact advice on how to keep your circle whole. The final chapter is filled with lists of inspirational music, books, and web pages for you to relish.

This book will help you create loving, supportive relationships in a circle of women, for it is within the Christian community that you will find peace and joy. May your circle be unbroken.

CHAPTER 1

The Busy Woman's Guide to Spirituality

Silence is golden, and so rare in our lives.
What a gift to have ten minutes all to ourselves.
Thank you, God, for making us wise women, ready to receive. Amen.
—*Patricia D. Brown,* Heart to Heart Guidebook: A Spiritual Journey for Women

One spring, quite a number of years ago now, I admitted to myself that I was not doing well when it came to friendships. My husband, two sons, and I had moved to New York City where I took a new position with a global church office. I knew almost no one. For all my love of my new work, the stress of the move was compounded by having to learn the ropes as a true amateur at how to get things done in a large institution. I felt a huge void that I soon realized was loneliness. While immediate family, colleagues at work, and neighbors kept me busy, I longed for someone with whom I could go deeper. I needed sisters who would not only enrich my life, but also save my sanity.

We women often come together in a hive of activity for worthwhile causes. Congregations swarm with busyness. Yet rarely do we slow long enough with one another to find the deep-seated spirit of renewal for which we desperately long. It is good for us to set aside time in our hectic schedules to pause and consider our lives. We want a place where we may slow down and examine what it means to be daughters of God. We seek a quieter place where there is an opportunity to listen intently to ourselves and to others.

This book is intended to help change the ways we get together as women. It is about what we can do when we gather specifically for the purpose of spiritual growth. It is for the multitude of us who seek a deeper spirituality in Christ—many of whom, for years, deny and repress what we know is true and live in contradictions, inviting internal conflict. Consequently, our lives become frantic. But as we join other women and turn our hearts to God, we experience a reorientation of values from deep within. Through the process of spiritual growth, we clarify our values, acknowledge our own unique gifts, and use our newfound knowledge to strengthen our relationships and our family in the larger community. With a gentle hand, this book demonstrates how women's Christian spirituality groups, or circles, may be a tool for discovering how the Holy Spirit is working uniquely in our lives: how God is working through us to be a channel of light and love to the world. The primary purpose of this book, then, is to help *you* begin your own women's Christian spirituality circle in which you and those gathering with you may develop your relationships with God and, at the same time, envision new ways to inspire, encourage, and affirm one another.

✳ What Is a Women's Christian Spirituality Circle?

Exactly what do we mean when we speak of a women's Christian spirituality circle? Here is some background information for you to think about.

The word *spirit* comes from the Latin *spirare,* which means "to breathe." In Hebrew, the word for "spirit" is *ruah,* which also means "breath." In essence, our spirit is what gives us life and breath. When we speak of spirituality, we are talking about that which connects us as humans to the life of God who is the breath of life that sustains the world.

Jesus tells an ancient story about wise and foolish women. Seven bridesmaids, thinking ahead, bring enough oil for their lamps to last the entire evening of the wedding celebration. Seven other bridesmaids do not. When the wedding is delayed, the foolish women ask those who were wise to share their lamp oil. But the wise women say no to this request. They realize that if they share their oil, they too will not have enough to last the night. Then the entire wedding party will sit in darkness.

The foolish bridesmaids decide to return to their homes to get more oil. But when they return, they realize they have missed the wedding entirely. Jesus is quick to point out the moral of this story to those who are walking numbly through life: "Keep awake!"

Spirituality is staying awake—alive and aware of our relationship with ourselves, with others, and with God. It is an intentional, awakened state that reminds us again and again that God has a deeper design on our lives than may appear on the surface. On this spiritual quest, we embark on a journey to make sense out of what might seem to be random or chaotic.

What, then, is this *women's spirituality* thing? Something "new age"? Another book club? The latest church growth gimmick? Women's spirituality groups may seem like a new idea to some, but the truth is that they are not.

✳ How Long Have There Been Women's Circles?

Throughout Christian history, women around the globe have come together in circles to pray and worship, to explore their relationships with God, and to celebrate the passages of their lives. Indeed, the founding of the first church in the ancient city of Philippi was begun by a circle of women. On Paul's missionary trip there, he encountered a group of women meeting outside the city gates. When Paul shared the good news of a liberating Jesus, the women, with the leadership of Lydia, an outstanding businesswoman, were moved to organize the first church in their city (Acts 16:11-15).

Since biblical times, women around the globe have gathered together to worship, pray, and sing. Similarly, women's circles have been a longtime tradition of church life. Women's circles create a haven—a place for us to be who we are, a place to explore our relationships with God and with one another, and to celebrate God's work in the everyday happenings of our lives. Together we come to understand our connection as daughters of Christ and then we reach out in service and mission.

Remnants of our grandmothers' Sarah Circle, Martha Circle, or Mary Circle remain today. Even now, in the midst of daily life, women gather in circles to quilt, to work on mission projects, and to study the Bible. In essence, we are reclaiming our "her-story." Old ways are being rediscovered and reinvented in our time to form women of spirit for greater service to the world.

Yet times have changed since our grandmothers' day—and even our mothers' day. The majority of us hold part or full-time positions. Women in the home caring for children, the elderly, and households have more demands than ever. Most of us no longer live in communities where children can walk to school and extracurricular activities. The volunteer work required to chaperone children's school field trips, help at the community bazaar, and work at the church office, once spread out over a large number of women, has been loaded on the few available women. This is why more than ever we need to take time from our busy lives to gather and connect with one another.

✳ What About the Guys?

Let me pause here to say a brief word about the opposite sex. It may seem contradictory to some that I would be advocating women-only groups when women finally are working alongside men in business occupations as well as in ministry. Nevertheless, I find these women's groups quite important. Even though I work alongside men in other avenues of my life, I yearn for a feminine oasis—a place where being a woman is the norm that is embraced and not just accommodated. I need a place to know myself with the support of women.

My hope is that we women today, like women throughout the ages, will feel confident in our own abilities to create sacred times and to invite others to join us. Together we will conceive a safe space for the Spirit to be formed in our lives.

✳ How Is a Women's Christian Spirituality Group Different from Support, Encounter, or Therapy Groups?

You may be wondering what the difference is between a women's Christian spirituality circle and other groups you may belong to, such as support, encounter, therapy, and recovery groups. Although all of these groups offer important vehicles for growth, yet subtle and profound differences exist

First, both recovery and therapy groups are problem oriented. People come to them to work on specific difficulties or even addictions. Their primary focus is on the pain of the past and obstacles to be overcome. What's more, their work is centered around the personalities in the group.

Women's Christian spirituality circles, while also intensely personal, are not focused on personalities. Instead, they are community centered. They allow women to explore, express, and develop their experiences and understandings of God and how God is at work in their lives. Just as praying, reflecting on biblical stories, taking a walk in the outdoors, singing, or reading inspirational books are tools for spiritual growth and nourishment, so too are women's spirituality groups an avenue for remembering who we are as baptized daughters of God. Christian spirituality circles most often are groups of women who want to deepen and celebrate God's presence in their everyday lives. Christian spirituality is not something separate from life but a new, deeper, and intentional way to live day by day.

Perhaps you have attended in the past what I label self-improvement or support groups. These groups meet to give support as participants lose pounds, gain parenting skills, or learn better marriage communication techniques. These meetings are an important source of teachings, information, and support.

Christian spirituality circles, on the other hand, need to take care not to distort spiritual work and gatherings, making them into another form of self-improvement. Self-improvement groups, articles, and books begin with the premise that there is something terribly wrong with us. They have us dwell on our "warts" instead of our "beauty marks." They propagate the belief that we can save ourselves. Whereas, in the work of the Spirit, God tells us to give up trying to save ourselves. Our saved state comes to us freely as we live in God's grace through Jesus Christ. God does not ask us to live up to magazine and movie images. We can be okay as we are, knowing that God is working within and through our lives.

Your circle will need to be clear about the kind of group you are in order to remain faithful to your core purpose. What makes women's Christian spirituality circles distinct from self-help, recovery, therapy, and support groups—as well as from a group of socializing friends—is that the central purpose for the circle's existence is to nourish the participants' spiritual development. Here is a quick rule of thumb to remember: Women's spirituality is more about celebration and less about recovery.

✳ Who Comes to a Women's Christian Spirituality Circle?

Because of their universal appeal, women's spirituality circles encompass all ages, from teenagers to senior citizens. Participants are women who are looking for a fresh word in spiritual growth. Some of these women also may be attracted to being part of a circle because of a new awareness of the need for female friendship.

Whom do you invite to be part of a new group? Anyone and everyone interested in deepening her spirituality. This resource is designed to help you create a circle for women of the Christian faith, but women of other faiths and women who are seeking faith will find the processes and guidelines within these pages meaningful and enlightening as well. Women's spirituality circles provide excellent opportunities for evangelism—easy ways to incorporate new women into the congregation's larger fellowship. Informal groups of women meeting in a neighborhood also will feel at home because of core spiritual teachings and an ecumenical emphasis. And let's face it: there are a lot of women who for various reasons have dropped out of church life. They have despaired of further change within the church and seek fulfillment in other venues. They, too, may find new meaning and clarity for their lives in a women's spirituality circle.

✳ What Happens in a Women's Christian Spirituality Circle?

Women throughout the church are developing programs of self-awareness designed to help them grow spiritually. They are combining creative energy, "mother-wisdom," and "sister spirit" to form informal spiritual growth circles. These circles are a safe place where women validate one another's concerns about life, love, family, and community, and offer the opportunity for venting. Participants also have many chances to enjoy lighthearted laughter. Whatever happens when the circle gathers, the women experience heartfelt care, because the circle is about their hearts being centered in God's love.

This book walks with you, step-by-step, to help you begin just this kind of women's spiritual growth circle in your own congregation, organization, or neighborhood. The notion of a circle of hearts comes from the Christian tradition that sees the heart as not only a physical part of the body but also as the center of the person, drawing together mind, body, and spirit. This book helps you develop the kind of group life that speaks to your hearts, which extend inward to God and outward to your families and communities.

Because no two women's circles are exactly the same, *the suggestions in this book are not hard and fast rules.* Instead, they are intended to guide your planning for a program tailored to meet the needs of your particular group. These guidelines may be adapted for use by small circles of as few as three or four, to large groups of one hundred or more. Whether your circle chooses to meet for an entire morning or evening, for an hour, or for thirty minutes, a significant outcome of your experience will be the affirmation that each woman is a holy child of God and is important in God's divine plan. Each of you is the beloved of God.

The model offered here is not laid out in a traditional student-teacher approach. Instead, it employs shared leadership, group interaction, and the sharing of stories. This book leads you and your group through an experience of peer ministry, self-discovery, mutual support, and prayer. Some of the suggested activities may require you to reflect on your present lives or to recover old memories. Other activities may push you to reassess your priorities. As a result, you will begin to live and serve in new ways—intentionally and deliberately.

There are four basic components found in most women's Christian spirituality groups: (*1*) *Sacred Stories* from the Scriptures teach the Bible in new ways to move and change lives; (*2*) *personal story-telling* encourages women to share their lives, identify their concerns, and see more clearly who they are and where they are going; (*3*) *down-to-earth practices* teach women to use the time they have for themselves and God—to slow down and place activities such as relaxation exercises, journaling, reflection, and quiet times in their daily lives; and (*4*) *prayer rituals* help women find their identity. For now, let us take an introductory look at each one; we will explore them in greater depth in later chapters.

1) Sacred Stories

Some of us sing, *"Thy word is a lamp unto my feet and a light unto my path,"* while others sing, *"I love to tell the story of unseen things above, of Jesus and his glory, of Jesus and his love."* We have in common the need for God's Word in our lives. That is why Bible study is a primary part of the spiritual journey. Because this book is about spiritual growth groups that help women seek and hear God's will for their lives while they get to know one another, Sacred Scripture and Christ-centered teachings are at its core. Using the four listening/reflective Bible study models found in chapter 5, participants not only will experience the biblical lessons but also will tell their own stories and bond as they gain insight into their place in the world.

2) Storytelling

We sit and read a gospel text for the umpteenth time when, finally, its words are able to penetrate our skulls. There, squarely in front of us, within that page of words sit our lives. We are the Samaritan woman—soon to be first woman evangelist—who met Jesus at the well, Mary who washed Jesus' feet, and the unnamed bent-over woman who was healed by Jesus. Through their stories we are empowered to open our mouths and to put into words, perhaps for the first time, our own precarious stories of faith.

Interacting with biblical stories naturally leads to talking about our personal stories. And we love to talk! Yet, as we draw on Scripture to make sense of our lives, this talk is not frivolous, but meaningful. Sharing our journeys can be a source of wisdom and insight for ourselves as well as for those within earshot. When we are the listener, we get to eavesdrop on another's experiences, and suddenly we don't feel quite as alone in our own feelings and realities.

In her book *Writing a Woman's Life,* Carolyn Heilbrun writes, "As long as women are isolated one from the other, not allowed to offer other women the most personal accounts of their lives, they will not be part of any narrative of their own. Like Penelope waiting for Ulysses, weaving and unweaving, women will be staving off destiny and not inviting or inventing or controlling it" (New York: Ballantine Books, 1988, 46).

We become more aware of how God is speaking to us when we tell our stories alongside the gospel story. When we give our full attention to others and to ourselves in non-judging ways—without commenting, interrupting, censoring, correcting, or even complimenting—we may truly hear, perhaps for the first time, not only our own voice, but also some new meaning of another's life situation. Suddenly, as we glimpse the repeated patterns of the years, our past becomes clear and the path before us is unveiled. We may even learn the lesson that has been desperately and repeatedly trying to awaken us from our sleep.

Some women's groups have adopted the use of an object such as a paperweight, cup, stone, or shell in the spirit of the native American "talking stick" tradition. The object is passed from person to person around the circle whenever it is time for storytelling or sharing. Only the woman holding the object is allowed to speak. She has the group's undivided attention. If you decide to use this idea in your circle, let me make three suggestions. (1) Use the same object at all meetings. (2) Choose something durable. (3) The object should balance in the hand and be pleasing to the touch.

Groups who use a talking stone, stick, or bowl find that it helps women focus their thoughts. Women finger it, turn it over in their hands, and look at it as they talk. Possession of the object does not mean a person has to share. When a woman doesn't want to speak, she simply passes it on silently to the next individual.

3) Down-to-Earth Practices

Praying, practicing relaxation exercises, creating a focus center, and writing in a journal are all things that give us balance and nurture our spiritual being. Each of these down-to-earth practices can be a meaningful part not only of your circle experience, but also of your everyday life.

Keeping a personal journal, for example, is both fun and meaningful. To be your true self—authentically *you*—you first must learn who you are in this moment of your life. Self-inquiry helps you clarify the internal dialogue you carry inside yourself. Through prayerful self-inquiry, you are guided "home" and aligned with the Holy Spirit who lives within you. This enables you to discern what part of the dialogue might be God's prompting.

A journal is a bit like the diaries we kept in a secret place as girls. Writing in our diaries was a way of sorting out who we were before sharing what we were thinking with our girlfriends. Likewise, a journal is the place where we can write secret thoughts and safely explore our most hidden, inner selves.

A journal is a gift we give to ourselves as well as to those we care for. Writing about life challenges, past and present, helps us gain clarity in our relationships with God, ourselves, and others. Over time, the patterns of acting, relating, and thinking all emerge. As we read and reread what we've written, we begin to see the choices we have made and how we have changed. The pages remind us of our inner beauty and humble us as we confront our frailties.

I keep a personal prayer journal. In it I reflect on my experiences, on the "places" I realize God is present to me. This invites me to express what is in my heart and to explore my creativity. As I write, I remember I am not alone. When I journal in prayer, I open my heart to the vulnerabilities that allow me to look at hidden parts of myself. I call upon God's Spirit for guidance, wisdom, and above all, compassion and mercy. I remember that I am of sacred worth. I find the peace that comes as I live in connection with my mind, body, and spirit.

In light of the highly personal nature of journaling, privacy is important. You will want to keep your own journal where it will not be read by another. Your journal will help you find your voice and prepare you to share with your circle. Remember, however, that you will share your journal with others in your circle *only as you choose.*

Another practice your circle will find helpful is the relaxation exercise. This means simply that you settle yourselves "down and in"—you relax in one another's company. First, light the candles on the focus center you've lovingly designed and constructed. Then close your eyes and take deep, soulful breaths for five minutes or more. Sit in the quiet or begin to unwind by making announcements, which may include information about upcoming events or gatherings as well as personal information about changes in your lives. Announcements are not incidental, but an integral part of your time together. Whatever ways or means you use, your goal is awareness of being in the present moment.

4) Prayer Rituals

The purpose of prayer ritual is to transform the heart of the human being. It is sacred drama in which you and God are both audience and participant. Robin Deen Carnes and Sally Craig, authors of *Sacred Circles: a Guide to Creating Your Own Women's Spirituality Group,* say it this way: "Ritual is the act of consciously opening ourselves to the presence of Spirit" (San Francisco: HarperSanFrancisco, 1998, 94).

Rituals, ceremonies, celebrations, and traditions are symbolic acts that signify special meaning to us. At their best, rituals serve as a catalyst to a powerful experience that opens us to new dimensions of spiritual awareness. Rituals deepen relationships within the gathered community, as well as with the Sacred.

A "Blessing Cup" is one example of a prayer ritual. Passing a "Blessing Cup" from one to the other while saying the words "You are the beloved of God," signifies that we claim the time and place as special. It is a celebration of the moment and of one another. In this book, we focus specifically on women's communities who want to establish such meaningful patterns of prayerful, worshipful, Christ-centered ritual.

✳ Be a Part of God's Ever-Widening Circle

This book aims to answer common questions about women's spirituality today. You'll find suggested outlines and ideas for circle gatherings, along with suggested administrative details. In addition, information on scheduling concerns, promotional materials, and a variety of forms and worksheets will help you get your circle up and running. Please remember, however, that this guide is not the last word on forming and sustaining women's Christian spirituality circles. As I write, I am well aware that the experiences of women are individually rooted in each person's culture, time, and circumstances.

These guidelines aim to be suggestive rather than prescriptive. There is no one-size-fits-all image for the relationships between God and women. Instead, this book is my heart-offering. I hope many women will be encouraged to join in God's ever-widening circle. Your group has the opportunity to open a new avenue to women that will empower and equip them to live in heart-centered ways. I am not asking you to follow me on blind faith. Instead, work with the questions and suggestions yourself. Take what is helpful and leave the rest. Trust your inner voice and your prayer life to tell you the truth as you claim spiritual responsibility and authority for yourself.

As you begin this journey, I encourage you to make a commitment to prayer. Prayer should center on a constant awareness of the holy within yourself and within each woman you encounter. Pray that as women gather together, the Holy Spirit will be at work, bringing clarity and a deepened spirituality.

I also encourage you to consider three things you will need to address as you create your own women's spirituality circle. First, you will want your circle to be a haven, creating an environment that fosters each woman's individual gifts for ministry. This calls for an arena in which women are free to become who they are—a significant alternative to the prefabricated identities provided within many of our religious institutions. Second, you will need to take time to celebrate the passages of life as well as to honor your various and different lives that have brought you to this juncture. Third, you will want to draw strength from the courageous women of biblical times such as Sarah, Esther, Ruth, and Mary, as well as from examples of faithful women in church history and tradition such as Hildegard of Bingen, Joan of Arc, and Clare of Assisi. Through such channels, women's circles can continue to foster discovery and growth not found elsewhere in our contemporary churches.

✳ Questions for Reflection and Action

1. What is Christian spirituality? How have understandings of Christian spirituality changed over the years? Write down your thoughts and discuss with a friend or with a group.

2. Have you ever been part of a women's group of any kind? What was its purpose? How did the group accomplish its goals?

3. Who are the biblical women who inspire you and give you power to live? What women in your own life have inspired you? Tell why.

CHAPTER 2

Core Characteristics of Women's Christian Spirituality Circles

A journey to the heart goes through territory that many before you have walked. You do not go alone.
—The Quest of the Woman in Search of Her Heart

Most women's spirituality groups in the Christian tradition have six core characteristics. As you read about them in this chapter, be aware of which ideas excite, inspire, and energize you. Observe your reactions and note what is triggered in your emotions and thoughts. These responses will help you form a vision and make decisions for your own circle. We'll consider the six characteristics in this order: prayer, rituals and celebrations, Sacred Stories, storytelling, shared leadership, and "the feminine within." Then, before moving on, we will consider how the very act of arranging ourselves in a circle is a distinctive and defining characteristic of women's groups.

✳ 1. Prayer

When we pray, we experience the truth that God lives both with us and within us. God is present to us. The breakdown in prayer comes when there is so much noise in our heads and so much confusion in our hearts that we are not present to God. Prayer is a matter of becoming aware of God's sacred presence in every dimension of life. Simply put, prayer is being in the presence of God.

In your circle, some prayers may be determined and planned as part of the lesson. These may be prayers written ahead of time. At other times, the circle may be awed as a new baby is born, or experience wonderment when a member makes a life-changing decision. Such times provide opportunities for spontaneous moments of prayer. Intuitively, from somewhere deep within, we turn to prayer to give thanks or to make sense out of the randomness that life appears to bring.

It is almost always appropriate, at any time during your circle gathering, to stop, take a time-out with God, and pray. Prayer may be either spoken or couched in a time of quiet. Here is a sample prayer that could be said after a woman has shared: "Dear God, we know that you have heard what Peggy shared with us. We thank you for her story. Continue to surround her with your steadfast love. Amen."

The group, having demonstrated compassion and care for Peggy, then may decide whether to move on.

You may come to the group feeling abandoned. Then suddenly you belong. You felt alone and isolated, but now, gathered in prayer with sisters, you see the profound reality that you are surrounded by God's care. When we pray, the circle is joined to all that has been, is now, and is yet to be. In prayer, we become coworkers and cocreators of our lives with God.

On a practical note, your circle may want to keep a notebook or note cards to remind you for whom to pray. Some circles make a daily prayer commitment to lift each member of their group between meetings.

✳ 2. Rituals and Celebrations

Prayer rituals are one important kind of ritual, but there are other meaningful rituals that circles may practice as well. Chapter 6 presents an in-depth discussion of this topic.

Ritual is an important action in nearly all women's spiritual lives. A common example of ritual is when churches light candles on Sunday morning, signifying the start of worship. A spirituality circle also may light a candle as a symbolic act signifying their claim to a special time and place. This candle marks the beginning of the circle's time together and reminds them of their purpose as a community.

Rituals may be created for any occasion: the conception of a child, the death of a spouse, or even the first day of summer. No occasion is too big or too trivial. Women's rituals also mark occasions particular to a woman's life cycle, such as the onset of a young woman's first menstruation or a menopausal woman entering into "sagehood." Other meaningful traditions spring up especially during holidays. These are your own special times and occasions. Rituals provide the opportunity to say, "We remember. We celebrate in our own special way." They create a sense of community and connect you to one another and to the Holy. Your group will decide which symbols or occasions have meaning and what actions have power and bring you strength. These will become your rituals.

When it comes to rituals or traditions that hold importance in the Christian faith, don't wander too far afield looking for rituals your circle may embrace. Christianity holds many rich traditions from centuries past and present from which you may draw. You may share the mark of the cross by tracing its lines upon the forehead of another. You may pass and drink from a cup of blessing, and wash one another's feet. A Christian tradition of the tenth century inspired one circle of women to use a string of knots and beads to pray the Lord's Prayer and other memorized pieces. Such prayers aided by prayer beads—berries, pebbles, or threaded disks of bone—became common in every part of Europe. As in ancient times, contemporary women use beads to assist them in prayer.

Relax and know that ideas for rituals will spring forth naturally from your gatherings. Choose the prayer rituals that are right for your group's specific situation. You'll discover, sometimes by trial and error, the kinds of prayer rituals to use in your group. The important thing is simply to include ritual—as simple as lighting a candle or as elaborate as putting movement to music—as part of every gathering.

✳ 3. Sacred Stories

Devotional reading of the Scripture has always been a wellspring of spiritual life. When combining biblical study with prayer, we open ourselves to God's works. We invite the Holy Spirit to pray *in us.*

Our goal in reading the Sacred Stories is not simply to learn the contents of a biblical text, but to grow into a deeper, more authentic relationship with

God. Through the Sacred Stories, God draws us into the divine self.

In chapter 5, I offer four methods of heart-centered Bible study: (1) Praying the Scripture, (2) Awakening Hearts, (3) Imagining, and (4) Responsive Listening. Not all study processes are equal, so you'll want to try all four in your circle to discover those which best meet the needs and personalities of your group. Alternating the four devotional processes will lend variety to your Bible study.

✳ 4. Storytelling

Women's spirituality is grounded in our experience as daughters of Christ: we are the beloved of God, created in God's image. Church theology and doctrine may play an active role in your circle's discussions and insights, but by and large, your circle will determine for yourselves what faith in Christ means according to *your experiences*.

Our spirituality is rooted in the daily encounters of what it means to be a woman. Whether we are at work or feeding a baby, cooking breakfast or attending Sunday worship, we are living out our spirituality as we interact with God's world. It is essential to remember that, for the most part, women do not think dualistically. That is, we do not divide God's creation, separating all things into two categories: one being the "sacred" and the other being the "secular." All is sacred and falls under God's care. This includes all people and their activities: the waitress as well as the missionary, the woman changing the baby's diaper as well as the woman singing in the choir.

Personal stories take many forms. Vivid stories of pain call for prayerful healing. Spontaneous narrations illustrate our common life and experiences. The stories that are shared in a group are more rich memoir than dry autobiography, more remembrance than fact. Yet it is these remembrances that open us to deeper dimensions of spiritual awareness. They serve as growing points that let us know we do not walk alone in the valleys. James B. Wiggins states poignantly that "the importance of stories lies ultimately less in what is told than in how whatever is told gets told" (*Religion as Story*. Lanham, Md.: University Press of America, 1975, 20).

Recounting personal sagas deepens relationships, both within the circle and with God. Of personal storytelling, Lesley A. Northup writes: "Thus, the sharing of personal biography leads to a chain reaction in which the collective story of the community—its myth—is developed. . . . Indeed, narrative is at the heart of how women understand themselves, express themselves, and create community among themselves" (*Ritualizing Women: Patterns of Spirituality.* Cleveland: Pilgrim Press, 1997, 75 and 84). It is our stories that form us and give us identity as a community.

In the story of *The Quest of the Woman in Search of Her Heart*, the character Sage reminds the wise woman, Questa, "Tragedy and disappointment enter every life. . . . Each person has at least one story that would break your heart" (112). We need the stories of women who overcome adversity, achieve success beyond their wildest dreams, and show courage in the face of hopelessness. We also need to hear and to tell our own tales of failure, disappointment, and heartache. Telling our stories, and hearing the "her-stories" of others, opens us to new vistas of understanding and possible action. (For a more in-depth look at storytelling, see chapter 4.)

✻ 5. Shared Leadership

Most women's spirituality groups consciously choose to operate with egalitarian models of leadership. The roles of leadership are rotated, shared, and minimized. Even when a woman is leading, she is unlikely to move from her place in the circle, to stand at a higher spot, or to take a position implying superiority or separateness. There often is no formal leadership structure and no designated teacher or leader. Instead, the women work together as a whole, just as women gather in a kitchen to prepare a meal, form teams at their place of employment to complete a project, or volunteer to accomplish a task. Each woman does her part in a way that fits who she is. Leaders who do evolve most often are not authorized by divine consecration or institutional pecking order, but by personality and skill and the immediate needs of the community.

Women's circles are, for the most part, nonhierarchical. In some ways, hierarchy is a familiar and therefore comfortable way to operate. But it has not always been a nurturing approach, especially for women.

Some groups have a general facilitator or contact person—perhaps the woman who originally organized the circle. In other groups, people take over the task of leader at different intervals depending on the needs of the community at any given time. Leadership roles include proposing direction, offering information, harmonizing for unity, encouraging, and offering alternative solutions. Designating a contact person for the life of the circle, or sharing the task week by week, may be helpful. This person also may be responsible for ordering resources and making sure they are on hand for the circle's gatherings.

Other circles rotate leadership to those who are willing to serve. Rotating leadership is a journey out of comfort and into growth. You may decide that your general facilitator will be responsible for determining the structure and content of your circle gatherings, making needed preparations, and facilitating the meeting itself. Some women may have particular skills to facilitate a group; nevertheless, it is important to allow everyone the opportunity to facilitate in her own style and then to honor her particular offering. Your circle may work out a leadership plan that suits your unique situation.

✳ 6. The "Feminine Within"

Women's Christian spirituality is in touch with what I call the "feminine within"—what puts us women in touch with the earth. We feel our bodily connections to the earth, and we try to live accordingly. As women, we operate with the understanding that we do not have dominion over the earth, as opposed to the mistaken notion that the earth exists for human exploitation. Instead, we hold a reverence for our interdependence with the earth and for our place and responsibility in God's creation.

Many of us view gardening as a spiritual practice.

We share an interest in herbs and flowers. Women's prayer rituals are earthbound—in close touch with nature. Your circle may want to meet in a garden, park, or someone's yard to remind you of the sacredness of God's good earth.

Women also feel at ease participating in body-prayer. We understand that it is good to use our bodies, to bring our whole person to God. This understanding comes from the reality that our bodies are a constant reminder of our earthiness. (For a good example of body-prayer, see chapter 6.) In women's prayer rituals, there is a respectful recognition of bodily processes created by God. Prayer rituals may celebrate God's gift of women's reproductive and nurturing powers. Monthly menstruation, pregnancy and birth, and menopause are seen as blessings and part of the Creator's plan.

We all have issues about our bodies to work through. Women's spirituality encourages us to appreciate our bodies as part of God's creation. This flies in the face of social conditioning that tells us our bodies are distorted and need to be changed, forced, and starved into submission to become the "ideal woman." As we esteem ourselves as gifted women of God, we care for our bodies through exercise and proper nutrition, which brings us back to our senses—literally. God teaches many lessons when we listen to our bodies.

Adele Wilcox, author of *Self and Soul: A Woman's Guide to Enhancing Self-Esteem Through Spirituality,* sums it up for us: "Self-care of the body directly impacts self-care of the self and soul. . . . When you finally get to the point where you love your body and treat it appropriately, you will no longer obsess about it. In fact, it will be so much a part of you that you will forget about it. It will be *your* body—your healthy, loving body, the temple that it is" (New York: Daybreak Books, 1997, 64 and 71). May that day come soon!

✳ Circle 'Round: A Woman's Way of Being and Doing

It is fitting to conclude this chapter on the core characteristics of women's circles with a discussion of the significance for women of a *circle*. When we long for community and long-lasting intimacy with other women, we instinctually arrange ourselves in a circle. Sitting in a circle, we share both leadership and responsibility. In this safe environment, we may speak not only of our experiences as women, but also of our feelings, needs, and yearnings. As we talk about things such as motherhood, seek to redress women's suffering, recall our ancestors, and share concerns about our relationships, we become teachers and mentors for one another, offering advice and wisdom. Because we women take delight in one another's company, we come together as we are, with our frailties and strengths, and leave the gathering different, more ready to cope with the outside demands on our lives. Lesley A. Northup summarizes the result when she writes, "This strategy is effective in helping women to redefine their religious selves positively, to present themselves as strong and outspoken religious leaders, and to understand themselves as crucial actors in the larger story of their faith" (*Ritualizing Women,* 101).

A circle of women, facing one another, is a distinctive departure from business as usual. It is certainly a change from the typical rows of church pews facing an altar where the "real" action presumably takes place. In contrast, the circle is a horizontal arrangement that makes the ground it circumscribes sacred. Instead of standing in front of the group, a position that would imply superiority or separateness, women fulfilling leadership roles remain seated in the circle. In the circle, undeniable power becomes available. Sitting in a circle is not only a sign of unity but also a specifically instrumental act, one that has direct repercussions on the surrounding community and world.

There also is a certain vulnerability in gathering in a simple circle of chairs. When we unite in a circle, we sit facing one another as equals. There is no outside agenda to distract our attention as we encounter one another knee to knee and eye to eye. What's more, a circle can expand infinitely to include more participants.

Circles represent focused energy and come from a number of deeply rooted metaphoric associations such as the womb, the moon, the earth, and even the baptismal font. Lesley A. Northup says of the circle, "The circle, then, is the dominant image . . . women's rituals tend to emphasize the cyclical—the recurrence of menstrual periods, seasons, moon phases, harvests; the endless cycle of life, death, and regeneration" (*Ritualizing Women*, 68). Forming ourselves in a circle, then, creates a sense of community and commonality. In the closeness of a circle, we strive to create an environment of camaraderie and support, both intellectually and spiritually. As a result, we discover pieces that are often missing from our lives: hospitality, support, and genuine community.

✳ Questions for Reflection and Action

1. As you were reading, which ideas excited, inspired, and energized you? Observing your own reactions, what was triggered in your emotions and thoughts? These responses may be helpful in forming a vision for your circle.

2. What are the important rituals and traditions in your life? Name or list them and tell why they are important.

3. What are the ways you stay in touch with your womanly earthiness?

CHAPTER 3

Birthing Your Circle

*I can't tell you how to find your heart. . . . Only you
know where it is. No one can make the journey for you.
Only you know the way back to your heart. But I can
walk with you.*
—The Quest of the Woman in Search of Her Heart

So you are ready to take the plunge and "conceive" your own women's Christian spirituality group. Congratulations! This chapter will help you do just that. But know that it is not written as the expert guide to creating the ultimate group. Instead, we, as in many other new challenges of our life, are "making it up as we go along." So trust your intuitive side and enter into this "pregnant" venture girded in prayer. Know that the Spirit is moving among you and your sisters in new ways.

❋ Midwife the Circle

First and foremost, *don't do it alone.* Find a friend to share the load. In this way, you can join your energies and creativity and bounce ideas off each other. Also, you can model the shared leadership that will later guide the group process. Besides, it is more fun to work on projects with a friend.

Once the group is established, your facilitating role will fade as others in the circle take ownership. In time, you will meld into an equal member alongside the others. So, if you are a person who needs to be in charge, make a deal with someone to give you cues when it is time to pull back. This will safeguard you from repeating old patterns that are unhealthy for you and unhelpful to sharing leadership.

✳ Create Interest

Begin by talking about the idea of a spirituality circle with friends. Although most women don't want to be the organizer of a group, many are willing to be part of a gathering and are grateful that someone else is organizing it.

Here are some ideas for finding women who might be interested:

• Start a new group or plug into meeting times of an already existing group.

• Put an announcement on the bulletin board at work, in the grocery store, or in a newsletter.

• Hold a get-together or party and send out invitations. (Read on for more details.)

• Call a few women and invite them to a first meeting or "Introductory Gathering."

• Secure a meeting site at a church, library, or community room; print and distribute flyers, and see who shows.

• Spread the news by word of mouth. Most groups come together through relationships.

✳ Extend the Invitation

As suggested above, one effective way to begin your circle is to extend invitations to specific women. (Various sample invitations ready for you to adapt and use are found at the end of this chapter.) Make phone calls to check out interest levels. Invite women in a way that does not make them feel they must attend so that they do not hurt your feelings. And don't invite people because *you* feel obligated not to hurt *their* feelings.

Invite between six and twelve women—or a few more, if you like, to account for those who may opt out because it doesn't fit their current needs. Generally speaking, smaller groups offer more intimacy, and larger circles, chosen with care, yield greater diversity. Your group may even number over one hundred. In that case, you would divide into a number of circles for activities that call for a smaller group setting, such as Sacred Story Bible Study.

A diverse group brings together women of varying ages and cultural backgrounds, both rich and poor, as well as women with divergent outlooks. Diversity can be your biggest strength as it stimulates ideas and understandings of the spiritual life.

✳ Put It in God's Hands

Prayerfully leave the final outcome of your group to God. In the end, trust that those who appear are the women who, in God's good will for each person's life, are to be there. Remember, once the circle becomes a reality, you are forming it not into *your* image, but *God's* image. Allow the group's relationships, dynamics, and processes to unfold as they will. Be open to the final composition of the group as well as to the fact that the circle will develop differently—and far more richly—than you ever imagined.

Finally, be realistic. Do not involve women who have deep emotional problems. Julia Cameron, in her book *The Artist's Way: A Spiritual Path to Higher Creativity,* calls these people "crazymakers." She writes: "Crazymakers are those personalities that create storm centers. . . . You know the

type: charismatic but out of control, long on problems and short on solutions. . . . Crazymakers like
drama" (New York: Jeremy P. Tarcher/Putnam,
2002, 44-45). I'm not saying these persons are not
worthy of our time, but the circle setting may not be
helpful for who they are. In the end, it would be
unloving both for them and for the circle to place
them in such a position. We would zap the energy of
the group trying to deal with their overwhelming
needs. (For more reflections on group and personality dynamics that might cause difficulties, see
chapter 8.)

✳ Check Out Assumptions

Once your group has gathered, there are some
decisions to be made. Don't just assume that everyone is on the same wavelength. Each woman needs
to clarify her assumptions and intentions at the
start. Otherwise, down the road people will be disil-
lusioned, anticipating one thing and getting something else.

To keep individuals from meeting at cross purposes, discuss what kind of group you want. Does
your circle have a particular focus? Will your circle
be an inward nucleus to do outward mission?
Perhaps your circle is a mother's-day-out group or
a single women's gathering with certain life-stage

needs. Is yours an "Artist's Way" circle, with spiritual creativity being the hallmark of the group?

Of course, you have a few "musts" as a Christian spirituality circle. Your core purpose is to walk more closely with Jesus. It also is understood that your gatherings will have two essential components: prayer and Sacred Scripture.

So you see, it is important to check out assumptions. Here are some important issues for you to consider.

Where should we meet?

Most women's groups I've worked with tell me that where they meet and how they arrange themselves to meet is very important. In her book *Ritualizing Women,* Lesley A. Northup points out that many groups gather in a domestic setting as a deliberate reaffirmation and sanctification of places that have been devalued and minimized in recent years due to the increasing number of women working outside the home. Indeed, women's ritual horizontally expands the definition of the sacred into areas previously considered profane—the home, the workplace, and nature. In this horizontal zone, women locate the sacred. "Wherever women work, love, gather, dream, remember, and relate" in God's name, we create sacred space (*Ritualizing Women,* 57).

Like the Samaritan woman learned from Jesus (John 4:1-42), wise women know that sacred space is not located solely in consecrated buildings or even on mountaintops. Worshiping women find the sacred in ordinary places—the kitchen, bathroom, or nursery, as well as the office, library, or factory. Nonchurch settings may be more comfortable for newcomers, especially if they aren't church-goers. Creating sacred space, then, is simply finding a place where we are comfortable to be ourselves—with one another and with God. You will want to give careful consideration not only to the setting you choose for your circle gatherings, but also to the environment you create within that setting. (For more on creating an inviting atmosphere, see chapter 4.)

Do we want open or closed membership?

You'll need to decide if your membership will be open or closed, and to what extent. Some, but not all, of your creative options include the following: (1) closing membership after the first few weeks; (2) adding a new member whenever someone leaves the group; (3) remaining open to new members as the Spirit leads; (4) opening your membership to new women during a predesignated time, perhaps in the fall.

Keep in mind that you are not an elite women's club, excluding others. You are a part of the Body of Christ. A core mission of your circle may be to reach out to other women to share what the group is discovering about God and about the worthiness of their own lives. The women's spirituality model is one of sharing talents, blessings, and works so that the community may be a place of healing and transformation for all women.

In the circles in which I have participated, welcoming new women into the circle has been essential to maintaining and sustaining the identity and health of the group. Your group also may want to look for ways to extend an open invitation to any and all women who might contribute to and benefit from your circle.

How do we introduce new members?

You will need to have a process for welcoming and introducing new members, especially if you choose to open the group once a year for new participants or to have open membership. Discern if the "fit" is right, both she for your group and you for her. You'll know. This is done not by vote but by mutual understanding and prayerful discernment. In this manner, the new member may enter and exit with grace. As women come and go from your group, trust that they are making the choice that is best for their lives at that time. A woman's choice to leave is not a betrayal or a personal rejection of you or of the circle. Honor her choice.

It is important to say a word here about comfort levels. Some groups are rigorous in their pursuit of spiritual holiness. They give and receive—sometimes harshly—constructive feedback, centered in the commitment that each person is striving to live to her full potential in Christ. Because women have differing comfort levels, you will need to gauge for yourselves the level of intimacy your group is prepared to take on, and communicate this to prospective or new members.

How are meetings scheduled?

Do you plan to meet weekly, monthly, quarterly, or even semiannually? Your circle should decide what day(s) and time(s) best fit your collective needs and schedules. Ask yourselves, "How much time do we honestly have and are we ready to commit?"

Some groups use a multiple group format. This is similar to the meeting plans used successfully by support groups such as Weight Watchers and Alcoholics Anonymous. Here is how it works. Plan to hold more than one gathering or meeting for each planned session or lesson. Participants then have the option of attending one of the numerous meetings scheduled each week, month, quarter, or so forth. This arrangement, which keeps groups from growing cliquish and encourages open membership, works particularly well in large congregations.

How much time do the meetings take?

In my experience, groups fill the time they have and leave important matters until last, no matter how much time is allotted. A great deal may be accomplished in thirty minutes, in sixty minutes, or in ninety minutes. Some groups may choose to meet for an entire evening. One group I know of meets for a full day each quarter. Another meets on Saturday mornings. Whatever your group decides, stick to your decision. Begin when you say you'll begin, and end when you say you'll end. If you run overtime, some members may need to leave before the closing. Staying on schedule helps everyone to be present from the opening until the closing of the meeting. Each member does her part by arriving on time and staying for the entire time. It is not fair to the others in the group if anyone regularly arrives late or leaves early. Even so, remember to live in grace for one another. There are always exceptions.

What if I miss some meetings?

We all have times in our lives when we cannot attend a meeting or event. We need to respect the demands of one another's lives and accept the fact that all of us have to make choices about what we can and cannot do at a given time. One circle made up of professional women who travel a great deal makes a special effort to welcome back those who miss gatherings. You, too, will want to find ways to help one another feel a part of the circle even when life's demands occasionally pull you away.

What about resources?

The resources you use will be determined by your circle's chosen focus or purpose, as well as by your particular needs or interests related to the essential components of prayer and Sacred Scripture, or Bible study. Lists of suggested books, music, and other resources are included in chapter 9. In addition to these kinds of resources, your group will need to consider what materials and equipment are necessary to create the desired meeting environment and atmosphere. Items for creating a worship center, for example, might include a candle, a small table and cloth cover or scarf, and any other objects or symbols that have meaning for the circle. All of the resources and materials may be kept in a central location or assigned room.

You may designate one person to acquire all the necessary resources and materials, and to assure that the resources are on hand for each circle gathering. Or, if you prefer, you may rotate this responsibility among circle members. You'll want to make the arrangements that best suit your group's unique situation.

What about food?

Food is an important issue for many women. Just ask them! Don't take the issue of food lightly. It's serious business. The decision whether or not to have food at your gatherings is entirely up to you.

Some circles show hospitality by serving refreshments as the women arrive or as they visit with one another at the end of the gathering. One group stopped having refreshments when it became a competition. The first week, a woman brought a home-baked cheesecake. From then on, the designated "hostess" felt pressured into playing the game "Can you top this?" The circle finally saw the monster they had created and stopped bringing food completely. They knew they wouldn't starve in one hour.

Another group has the guideline that only fresh fruit and veggies, or some other nutritious, energy-boosting food, may be served. Still another circle decided that all goodies must be store-bought. In other circles, some women decide to go out for coffee or a meal *after* the gathering.

I find it best to eliminate food altogether from the circle gathering. I don't need the temptation. And besides, who has time to remember to pick something up from the bakery? Here's the bottom line: whatever you decide, try it for a while and then evaluate your decision. Your preferences may change as your group develops.

What about children?

There are a number of creative options for welcoming mothers and their children into the circle. First of all, make mothers with children feel welcome. View children's interruptions as part of the weave of the gathering. There are many ways to do this. Be sure to childproof the location. Designate a particular gathering at which children are especially welcome, or at which childcare is provided. Or you may choose to provide childcare at every gathering. Some groups find a volunteer to care for the children at the site or in her own home. If child-care outside of the meeting is preferred, consider collecting dues to pay for a caretaker.

Whatever arrangements you make, remember that childcare is the responsibility of the entire community. Share any expenses. If children are accommodated, mothers with children will attend.

✳ Questions for Reflection and Action

1. What kind of group do you want to be a part of? What characteristic or component is an absolute for you? What is not critical?

2. What kind of commitment are you able and willing to make? Six weeks, six months, a year, or more?

3. Are you open to diverse understandings of the Christian tradition, or do you expect circle members to have similar perspectives? Why do you think you feel this way?

4. Finally, make a list of women you might invite to be part of a group, decide how you'll contact them, and get started. Seize the day!

✳ Sample Information Sheets, Invitations, and Announcements

Because you are a busy person, I know you will appreciate practical help for getting your group up and running. Following are six sure-fire samples you may use as is or adapt: (1) a single sheet handout to distribute to friends, (2) an announcement for a platform presentation, (3) a letter of invitation, (4) an announcement for a bulletin or newsletter, (5) an invitation to a circle gathering, (6) an announcement brochure.

INFORMATION HANDOUT

This handout gives a quick overview of a spirituality circle to those who want to know more. Use the handout at your initial meeting, or distribute copies to women who show interest.

CIRCLE OF HEARTS

A Time Apart for Women

A Circle of Hearts is a time for women to:

- Come together in a relaxed time

- Share their stories
- Sort out their lives
- Reassess God's will

Each gathering includes:

- Prayer rituals that touch you soul and help you find your identity
- Sacred Scriptures that move your heart and change your life
- Conversations in which you identify your concerns and cares
- Thoughts that help you see more clearly who you are and where you are going
- Spiritual disciplines such as keeping a journal, practicing relaxation exercises, praying, and claiming quiet times

You will leave with:

- Friends who support but do not meddle
- A deeper experience of God
- Down-to-earth practices to carry with you and enliven your daily life

PLATFORM PRESENTATION ANOUNCEMENT

When this announcement is made, have in place a display table staffed with someone who is ready to answer questions and register women as they leave the assembly. Have samples of the materials and resources you plan to use available for browsers. This platform presentation can be used during worship announcement times, coffee hours, or luncheons. You also might use this presentation in conjunction with a sample or introductory circle gathering.

Good morning. I am *(your name)*. I have been a member of this *(congregation/organization)* for *(number of years)*. I have *(tell about your family, such as: "A four-year-old daughter, Lauren")*.

I want to tell you about a special, new spiritual growth group for women that we are starting here at *(name of congregation/organization)*. It is called Circle of Hearts.

As you may have read in the bulletin *(or newsletter)*, Circle of Hearts is an ongoing program in which women come together to pray, study Sacred Stories *(hold up the Bible)*, and share concerns that affect our lives.

There are three heart-stirring things about the circle that I look forward to. First *(hold up one finger)*, I'll have a chance to talk with other women about the strain of being a woman. Some of us juggle kids, home, and work. Still other women go to school full time. Others of us are single, married, widowed, or divorced. This program invites women of all stages of life to meet in a relaxed, comfortable way.

Second *(hold up two fingers)*, I'll be able to step back and get a new perspective about what I'm doing with the precious little time I do have, and then begin to make decisions about how I *really* want to live.

Third *(hold up three fingers)*, I'll be able to be myself, to learn about myself, and to grow spiritually. I will discover how being *me* is a special ministry to others.

With *(name of committee chair, sponsoring group, or pastor)*, we are holding an open introductory gathering on *(day and time)*. We will meet in the *(location of building and room)*. I invite you to register for this introductory meeting. Please register today so that we may plan for the number who will be coming. You may also bring a friend by calling the number in the bulletin. Childcare will be available.

Please pray that this new ministry will grow and bless our entire *(church/organization)*. There is further information at the display in the *(location)* where you may register as you leave today. We hope you'll join in the circle.

INVITATION LETTER

Send this letter to prospective women partici-pants. The letter invites women to an introductory meeting where they may decide if the circle is right for them. Adapt it to fit your particular situation.

Date

Dear *(name)*,

Do you feel as though your life has become too hectic? If you are like me, you need to remind your-self to: Stop.

Look around.

And remember; this is the good stuff.

I invite you to be a part of an exciting new spiritual growth group for women. It is called Circle of Hearts. Circle Hearts is an ongoing program in which you will come together with other women to pray, read Sacred Stories, and share concerns that affect your lives. There are three reasons to take time now to attend the circle:

- First, let's face it: it's hard being a woman. Some of us juggle kids, home, and work. Other women go to school full time. Still others of us are single, married, widowed, or divorced. This program is for all women to meet in a relaxed, comfortable way and look at our strains and joys together.
- Second, you'll have the chance to step back and get a new perspective about what you are doing with the precious little time you do have. You'll get a chance to make decisions about how you really want to live your life.
- Third, you'll be able to be yourself, learn about yourself, and grow spiritually. You'll discover how being *you* is a real blessing to others.

A thirty-minute *(or sixty-minute)* open introductory meeting is being held on *(day and date)* at *(time)*. We will meet in the *(location of building and room)*. If you get a chance, please give the planners a call or e-mail so they may plan for the approximate number attending. Here are their names and numbers *(contacts' names and telephone numbers or e-mail addresses)*. If you don't get a chance to call, come anyway, and bring a friend or neighbor. Childcare will be available.

Don't say you can't do one more thing. Come find out if this is the answer for you. **Circle of Hearts may be one of the most important things you can**

do for yourself and your spiritual health. We hope you'll come.

Blessings,

(name and signature)

BULLETIN AND NEWSLETTER ANNOUNCEMENT

CIRCLE OF HEARTS

A Time Apart for Women

Circle of Hearts is a program that invites women to come together in a relaxed way to share their stories, sort out their lives, and reassess God's will. Each meeting includes prayer rituals that touch the soul, Scriptures that enliven daily life, and thoughts that help you see more clearly who you are and where you are going. You will leave with friends who support but do not meddle, a deeper experience of God, and down-to-earth practices to carry with you.

A thirty-minute *(or sixty-minute)* open introductory meeting *(or initial meeting)* is being held on *(day and date)* at *(time)*. We will meet in the *(location of building and room)*. If you get a chance, give the planners a call or e-mail so they may plan for the approximate number attending. Here are their names and numbers: *(contacts' names and telephone numbers or e-mail addresses)*. If you don't get a chance to call, come anyway, and bring a friend or neighbor. Childcare will be available.

CIRCLE GATHERING INVITATION

This invitation also may be adapted and used for an introductory or initial circle gathering. It is written for multiple group circle gatherings. See page 00 for a review of the multiple group format. You may adapt it to meet your particular needs.

CIRCLE OF HEARTS

Come with us on a journey to the Heart

You are invited to Circle of Hearts

Circle of Hearts is a creative, ongoing program that will help you grow spiritually. It is a gentle program of self-awareness and an awakening to the spirituality of women. You will have the opportunity to clarify your values, claim your giftedness, and enjoy genuine community.

Both thirty-minute and sixty-minute programs are forming. You may attend the gathering that best suits your schedule. The dates, times, and locations are listed here. Please sign up so that adequate resources and childcare may be available.

Date: *(day and date)*

Place: *(location)*

Time: *(times you will begin and finish)*

Cost: *(insert cost here)* per person

RSVP: *(insert telephone number)* Please reply as soon as possible. Let us know if you need any assistance to attend. We want you to be part of a Circle of Hearts.

BROCHURE

Make an attractive brochure for distribution. This sample promotes the multiple group format. You will want to reword it to fit your particular needs.

CIRCLE OF HEARTS

Circle of Hearts is the name given to an innovative program designed to help women grow spiritually. Created over coffee at a kitchen table, it is now spreading across the nation. Circle of Hearts successfully brings about a sense of belonging, hospitality, faith-sharing, and genuine community to women.

The purpose of Circle of Hearts is to lead you and a group of women meeting with you to greater self-awareness and to awaken you to God's Spirit in your lives while teaching you new ways to inspire, encourage, and affirm one another. Through this process of spiritual growth, you have the opportunity to clarify your values, claim your own giftedness, and return these new strengths to your family relationships and to the larger community.

The circle begins with a twelve-week journey (if you are beginning by using the resources *Heart to Heart Guidebook: A Spiritual Journey for Women* and *From the Heart Journal*) that leads your group through an experience of peer ministry, self-discovery, mutual support, and prayer. You will share your stories and bond by gaining insight into your current missions in the world. You also will experience an important element missing from many of today's churches: hospitality.

A Personal Prayer Journal

Explore the dynamics of discipleship as they apply to you: self-acceptance, stress, spirituality, feelings, personal growth, and friendships. Your journal guides you in reflecting on your experiences, preparing you to share your story, and helping you to realize the sacredness of your call. Journals can be formal or informal, guided or free form; they can be filled with poems and drawings as well as thoughts and reflections. Choose the style of journal that is right for you. You may use your journal independently at home and/or as part of sharing and discussion in the circle.

Circle of Hearts is a time for you to:
- Come together with other women in a relaxed time
- Share your stories
- Sort out your lives
- Reassess God's will

Each meeting includes:
- Prayer rituals that touch the soul
- Scriptures that enliven your daily life
- Thoughts that help you see more clearly who you are and where you are going

You will leave with:
- Friends who support but don't meddle
- A deeper experience of God
- Down-to-earth practices to carry with you

Circle of Hearts is sponsored by *(name of the sponsoring organization).*

You won't spend long hours getting ready for the lesson. Circle of Hearts understands the busy woman's schedule. Each person attends as a guest.

No one woman is a designated teacher or leader. Instead, you work as a whole. Just as women gather in a kitchen pulling together a meal or work with a team to accomplish a goal, each woman does her part in a way that fits who she is.

Frequently Asked Questions

✳ Where will we meet?

Anywhere two or three are gathered. It can be in a kitchen, church, home, restaurant, library, or work break room. Anywhere women are comfortable.

✳ How long is a gathering?

You can be in and out in thirty- or sixty-minutes *(state your designated time).* Your circle is designed so that you have the option of either a thirty- or sixty-minute gathering *(or whatever time you have decided)*. Either way, you leave renewed and ready to face the world again.

✳ How do we keep track of one another?

A sign-in sheet is kept. Mark the sheet upon arriving.

CHAPTER 4

Opening Moments to the Final Amen

In our final minutes together, with triumphant hugs goodbye, I saw it laid out. For a split second, celebration merged past, present, and future into a cohesive whole. Each one of their stories became my story. Through them I gained a new understanding of the past and present to carry me into my future.
—The Quest of the Woman in Search of Her Heart

Y ou sit facing one another in the circle you've arranged. *Now what?* I knew you would ask, so here is a chapter containing loosely woven steps to guide you.

✳ Your Initial Gathering

In many ways, the birth of a circle is like the birth of a child. First and foremost, it is a life-changing event. When a circle of women is lovingly, prayerfully called into being by those who desire to be spiritually formed into the image and ways of Christ Jesus, the path or "birth canal" is made for the Holy Spirit to unleash power for surprising change. The energies spiral outward from the simple circle, extending into the rest of our lives and into our families, communities, and the world. We literally affect the lives of our children and our children's children by gathering together!

You might say that your initial gathering is like seeing your baby for the first time. All the days, weeks (when you are spiritually hungry, a week can seem like a year!), or months of anticipation and preparation have passed, and you are ready for delivery. Your circle has arrived! Here are a few practical suggestions to help you make this special occasion all that it should be.

Begin in gentle ways that show hospitality. Take time to introduce yourselves. Use name tags. Invite each woman to tell something about the meaning of her name or share a story about how she came to have her name. Here's another suggestion: cut out descriptive words from magazines, such as *beautiful*, *forlorn*, or even *chocolate*. Invite participants to choose one or more words that say something about themselves and tape the words to their name tags. Then go around the circle and invite each woman to tell why she chose the word or words. Another idea is to ask each person why she has come and what she is looking for. Or invite the women to write down five significant spiritual experiences in their lives and choose one to share with the circle. Use your imagination and come up with your own creative starters. The possibilities are endless.

Review the principles that will guide your group. Read aloud the Be-Attitudes found in chapter 7 and answer question number one at the end of the chapter. Continue discussing until you have reached agreement concerning the one or two Be-Attitudes you consider vital for your group. As you welcome newcomers in the days ahead, ease them into the "group norms" by reviewing the Be-Attitudes with them.

Make basic decisions about your circle's arrangements at your first gathering. Let chapter 3 guide you through the decision-making process and help you check out individual and group assumptions. Decide together when and how the circle will introduce new members. Determine when and where you will meet. Other questions to sort through include: whether to serve food, whether to use prayer journals, and how you as a community will care for children. Lay out the options and begin to discuss what each person needs in order for the circle to work for her. Keep in mind that any decision may be changed at a future point as the group coalesces.

Use the "KISS" method of circle meetings: "Keep It Simple, Sisters." Share the tasks of making arrangements and doing logistical work. Keep preparations to a minimum.

✳ Planning Your Gatherings

Each of your circle gatherings will follow a basic format, although there will be some differences. To help you plan, I've divided the typical gathering into six sections or steps. After introducing each step, I share some basic guidelines to get you started.

STEP 1. Circle Your Hearts

In this first step, you gather around a central table, greet one another, receive your name tags, and arrange the objects on the table to create a focus center.

Room Arrangements

Plan to meet in an area where there will be few interruptions. The room should be large enough for you to gather as a full group as well as break into smaller groups as necessary.

You'll want to create an appealing environment for your gathering room. The best room setup consists of comfortable chairs arranged in a circle around a table—but not pulled up to the table. Create an attractive focus center on the table. This will remind each of you why you have come: so that God's Spirit will live more fully in you.

Creating a visually rich focus center provides space for you to express the spiritual part of your circle. When creating your circle's focus center, I suggest you select attractive materials. An easy arrangement can be made using a drape of fabric, perhaps an afghan or a pretty scarf or shawl from your dresser drawers. Place a lighted candle on the table as a reminder of the Holy Spirit's presence. Use quality candles. Choose other symbols that help draw and center you on God. Find some items that you love, that make you feel close to God. Arrange all of the items in a way that feels right. Spending time with it will let you know what else is needed.

On a focus center I created recently, I used a tan silk scarf with printed sea shells. On top I placed sun-bleached scallops from a day at the beach. The scallop is an ancient symbol of baptism. A bowl of water completed the setting. We used the water to bless one another and remember our own baptisms as we renewed our covenant with God and one another.

A focus center opens up the possibility of awe

and wonder to envelop your group. It is a physical space where the Divine may be glimpsed and experienced. Creating sacred spaces wherever your circle meets reaffirms your spiritual strength and enhances your relationship with God. Building a focus center acknowledges the sacredness of any space you inhabit, including your circle. It points to the Something Greater who exists beyond your own limited lives.

In this day, when we are accustomed to taking in the world though visual images and pictures, tangible focus centers make sense. Whether it be simple or elaborate, make your focus center a reflection of your love for God each time you gather.

Creating a Warm Space

Welcome the women as they arrive. Make them feel free to come dressed as they are—whether they're wearing jeans, workout gear, or a business suit. Remember, you are coming together in a relaxed way to share stories, sort out your lives, and reassess God's will for yourselves—not to show off the latest fashion.

Playing sacred music in the background as you gather and greet one another helps set the mood. Have someone play soothing melodies and hymns on a piano, guitar, or other instrument—or bring a

CD player and compact disks. Selections by the artist Enya and Celtic instrumental melodies are some of my personal favorites. I've listed other suggestions in chapter 9. Remember to play music again at the end of the meeting as you visit and prepare to leave. Be creative—and not too "churchy"—in your choices.

Name Tags

Use name tags for everyone attending, even if the women in your group know one another. This reminds all of you that your circle is not an exclusive clique; rather, you always remain open to God's entrance through a new person. Name tags help you learn one another's names quickly, particularly if you are using the multiple group format discussed in chapter 3. Name tags also enable you to attend the meeting each week or month that best suits your schedule without feeling alienated because you do not know everyone.

Use sturdy plastic holders for your name tags, so that you may reuse the name tags each time you gather. These are inexpensive and are available at your local office supply store. You can make your own attractive name tags to put in the holders. Print names in big bold letters so that they may be read easily. Do not use stick-on name tags. They are temporary and communicate this message to the persons receiving them. Be sure to have extra name tags on hand for new participants and visitors.

STEP 2. Heartwarmers

The second step of your gathering involves prayer and relaxation. With music playing to set the mood, begin with a simple prayer ritual. (See chapter 6.) Light a candle on your focus center. Call the circle into being by reading or saying a brief prayer, reminding all of the Spirit's presence. Read a brief Bible passage, play a special musical selection, or share a favorite quotation or short poem to focus the group.

In addition to prayer, relaxed breathing helps women make the shift to a more responsive attitude. Sit in silence for a full minute or lead the group in a relaxation exercise. First, place your feet flat on the floor; then take three deep belly breaths to relax and center yourselves.

Practical Tips for Prayer Rituals

Prayer rituals are enacted practices and prayers that carry deep spiritual meaning for the community. Chapter 6 gives guidelines for creating and using prayer rituals, as well as some suggested prayer rituals to try. What follows are a few practical tips to help you use prayer rituals effectively.

• Put people at ease by using simple and clear directions for interacting with one another.
• Make sure everyone understands the process before proceeding.
• Use good planning, so that you begin and end in the time designated.
• Use language that respects all experiences and mirrors the diversity of those represented.
• Carefully orchestrate the rhythm of the prayer ritual. Balance sound and silence, reflection and action.
• Be open to the spontaneity of the Spirit. God will move in greater ways than you ever imagined or dreamed.

STEP 3. Heart-Centered Story

The third step or section of your gathering is a time when you tell your stories and share your lives. You will share stories in personal, prophetic, powerful, preserving, and poignant ways: **personal**—subjective memoirs; **prophetic**—experiences that open you to new dimensions of spiritual awareness; **powerful**—rituals inspire courage, hope, and new ways of living; **preserving**—allowing the recitation of one another's history; and **poignant**—prayer rituals open you to a deeper relationship with the community and with God.

When we tell our stories, memory is created, enlivened, and celebrated. One woman's story evokes memories in another. In a chain reaction, the collective story of the community is developed. Each story becomes *our story*, opening new vistas of understanding and giving a corrective view of reality.

When doing personal storytelling, begin by reading aloud a prompting question. Then allow time for everyone to carefully reflect on the question. You may want to journal in silence for ten minutes before sharing.

What is a prompting question? Simply put, it is a question that leads you to share your stories. The question should be clear and concise. Word it in a way that is nonthreatening and that invites individuals to stretch. The question's purpose should be to help each woman be in touch with her feelings and experiences. It also should fit the theme and flow of the gathering. Sometimes you will find it necessary to use a series of prompting questions; other times you will want to follow the question with a clarifying statement or instruction. Here are some of my favorites:

• What Scripture comforts you, challenges you, or convicts you, and why?

• When have you found healing and wholeness in the midst of brokenness? When have you been blessed by reaching out to someone in a difficult season of her life? How were you healed, and how did you aid others in their need for healing?

• What prayer practices did you use as a child? How do you pray today—*really?*

• When have you felt that you were fully alive and that God was blessing you?

• Can you think of one to five events in your life when you felt God's presence? These are times when you felt God very near and close to you. They may have been spiritual mountaintop highs or simply ordinary times in your life. List them on a piece of paper.

• What was your church and religious experience growing up?

• When was a song precious to you? Even when you hear it now, it lifts your spirits.

• Can you think of three women, living or dead, who have found a "still more excellent way"? These are women who center the use of their gifts in love, who know God's purpose for their lives, and who live in that assurance. In all that they do, they bring glory to God. Who are they and why do you admire them?

These are all good topics for circle storytelling and reflection. Remember, as James B. Wiggins said, when autobiography is employed, *what* gets told is less important than *how* whatever is told gets told. Got that?

STEP 4. Opening Your Heart to Sacred Story

Now we come to Sacred Story Bible Study, a primary part of your circle's time together. Because this is so important, we've devoted an entire chapter to the matter, chapter 5. This chapter offers four methods of Sacred Story Bible Study, as well as suggestions for choosing effective Scripture texts. These approaches are not of the historical-critical methods of study. Instead, they are a spiritual exegesis of the text relating to the individual's discipleship walk.

Each biblical story holds a special lesson for the heart. As noted in chapter 5, the gospel stories are particularly fruitful to Sacred Story Bible Study. Follow the path of Jesus with the women and men who encounter him within the books of Matthew, Mark, Luke, and John and your heart *will* be touched.

STEP 5. HeartSongs: Writing to Your Heart

The next step in the gathering process involves using a journal. Writing in a journal prepares and guides us to reflect on our experiences, to sort out our thoughts, to clarify our values, and to share our stories. Many circles write in personal prayer journals for five to ten minutes during their gathering, as well as take time to journal on their own between gatherings. (For a review on journal writing, see chapter 1.)

Each person in your circle may keep a private journal. Blank journals may be purchased from a discount or stationary store. Nicer bound journals may be found in a bookstore. I like my journals to be special, and I have had journals of all sizes and styles.

Many women are intimidated by the blank sheets of paper that stretch out in front of them. They may prefer using a guided journal. A guided journal provides specific questions to answer and topics to think and write about. I've written a guided Christian journal titled *From the Heart Journal: A Personal Prayer Journal for Women* (Nashville, Tenn.: Dimensions for Living, 1999), which also may be used with the group resource *Heart to Heart Guidebook: A Spiritual Journey for Women*. Although I've seen a few nonreligious guided journals, this is the only Christian-focused guided journal that I know is on the market. It offers helpful guidance through the use of Scripture reflections followed by questions such as *What has fallen through the cracks in your life?* and *What changes would you like to make if you could? From the Heart Journal* asks you to write a letter to God, and to write a letter from God to you. The journal page asks, *What would God say?*

Writing your reflections and prayers ahead of your circle time prepares you to share with your friends in ways that are thoughtful and comfortable for you. Remember, however, that you share your journal with others in your circle *only as you choose.*

STEP 6. A Hearty Good-bye

The last step of your circle gathering sends you on your way. You want to leave the circle with a light heart, but also with lots to think about. Share a prayer, Scripture, poem (not too lengthy), symbolic action, prayer ritual, or reflective word. You might choose to use a guided prayer or a body prayer. Closing prayer rituals remind us who we are and "whose we are" as we reenter the world renewed.

Before leaving, the group should set the date, time, and place for your next gathering. What "final word" do you want everyone to leave with? Depart with a closing blessing.

✱ Your Circle Is Unique

Here is an important final word about your circle gathering: each group is unique. Let your gatherings reflect the special women you are. Some women's groups add more music or prayers. Others find a ritual that is special to them and repeat it at each gathering. Still other groups use more visual imagery or decorate their focus centers in colorful, artistic ways. In other words, don't be afraid to veer away from the gathering plan. God's Spirit is creative!

✱ Questions for Reflection and Action

1. Plan an outline for a circle gathering. Make sure you write the number of minutes allotted after

each directive so that you can estimate the total amount of time you'll need.

2. Make a list of books, music, videos, and other resources you might use with your circle. Then move on to my suggested list in chapter 9, "Resources for Your Circle," to add some more.

CHAPTER 5

Sacred Story Bible Study

One more thing before you go, . . . As you search for your heart, remember to look to God's guidance. Some people call this guidance the Holy Spirit, God's Spirit. It is this Spirit of Guidance that will tell you what to look at in yourself. Guidance will not always give you loud, step-by-step instructions. Instead, Questa, pay attention to the small voices. Then you will be attuned to God's Guidance. You may be surprised to discover God's Spirit of Guidance in both the miracles and in the ordinary places of life. They are the same thing, you know.

—The Quest of the Woman in Search of Her Heart

Devotional reading of the Scriptures has always been a wellspring of the spiritual life. Biblical, Christ-centered teachings are also at the core of the women's Christian spirituality movement—but perhaps in a different way than you've experienced in the past. As noted earlier, our goal in reading the Sacred Stories is to grow into a deeper, more authentic relationship with God—not simply to learn the contents of a biblical text.

As we open ourselves to God's work through the Scriptures, we invite the Holy Spirit to pray *in us.* Madame Guyon, a Christian woman of the seventeenth century, wrote about learning to pray the Scriptures in this way: "Of course, there is a kind of reading the Scripture for scholarship and for study—but not here. That studious kind of reading will not help you when it comes to matters that are divine!"[1] It may be interesting to know where the biblical region of Samaria is located on the map when reading of Jesus' encounter with the Samaritan woman, or to study the original Greek to learn the exact meaning of a word, or even to read the different variations of the Mary story found in the four Gospels; but this kind of intellectual study is not the emphasis when what you are seeking is a deeper walk with Christ.

Sacred Story Bible Study is a unique way for women—many of whom may be new to biblical stories—to experience the power of the Gospels in an interactive, spiritually nurturing way. Longtime students of the Bible also will hear God's word again in a refreshing way. The four Sacred Story Bible Study methods presented in this chapter create an intimacy that is authentic and that respects the authority of each person's voice as she considers God's work in and through her life. The methods grow more

---

1. Madame Guyon's writings are excerpted from *Experiencing the Depths of Christ* by Jeanne Guyon. Published by SeedSowers in Jacksonville, FL 32206.

powerful with each use—not because of good technique or excellent participation, but because the Spirit of God breaks hearts open. The gospel has transforming power!

✳ Origins of Sacred Story Bible Study

Monastic practices call the four methods of Sacred Story Bible Study presented here *collatio*, originally meaning "the bringing together" of a shared supper. It is a gathering of friends and stories around a table, bringing connections related to a Scripture text. The approach helps women to receive the Sacred Story and to share their own faith stories, thereby creating "common-unity" among people of diverse backgrounds.

These small group practices and variations have been widely used by churches around the world, by retreat groups, by workers on lunch breaks, and by Christians in developing countries where Bible study, prayer, singing, personal compassion, and social action often merge into one. This approach to Bible study also has been called the African Method or the Oral Tradition Approach.

✳ Guidelines to Help You Get Started

Before you begin Sacred Story Bible Study, let

me offer some simple guidelines that will help your circle get the most from your study.

First and Foremost, Listen

Listening, not talking, is the key. Group *lectio divina,* which means "divine reading," emphasizes hearing the message of the text, listening to others' reflections, and taking to heart what God is saying to each of you as an individual as well as to the circle as a whole. These methods are different from a discussion group. They emphasize listening and reflecting on the sacred text in order to help you grow in God's Spirit.

Manage Your Group Size to Stay on Schedule

If you are meeting for an hour, Bible study should account for approximately half of your time together. Each Sacred Story is designed to take twenty to thirty minutes when working in small groups of three to five women. (Add five minutes for each additional woman.)

When there are more than five participants in the full gathering, you will want to divide into smaller circles for the Bible study in order not to exceed thirty minutes. Fewer than five women in a group will help you to manage your time effectively and will allow direct participation by each person. It is important, however, that you have a minimum of three women in each group. Note that one circle of five within a larger gathering of several smaller groups may extend the time, causing other groups to wait needlessly. Whatever you decide, here's a rule of thumb: smaller is better. You also may find it beneficial to form your small groups by grouping together women who know one another the least.

Set Up Your Room

When five or fewer women are in the full group, you will remain seated around a central table—your focus center—for the entire gathering. (Review chapter 4 for more details about creating focus centers.) If your gathering is larger than five women, you will divide into multiple circles when it is time to share the Sacred Story. You will, however, remain and work in the same room. Space the groups around the room so that the women in each group may hear one another clearly. Women with hearing difficulties may ask their groups to move to a quieter space.

Circle your chairs into small groups and sit knee to knee. Unless you have only one small circle sitting around a focus center, do not circle your chairs around a table. This only places a barrier between you instead of creating the rich intimacy you seek.

Begin in a Welcoming Manner and
Choose a Facilitator

After circling your chairs and sitting knee to knee, start with introductions all around. If you already know one another, take a moment to exchange greetings. Then negotiate together who will serve as facilitator, the one who will convene your group and lead you through the entire study. It is best if this leadership role is passed to a different woman for each new Bible study session. If you are breaking into different small groups each time, this should happen naturally.

Another way to choose a facilitator is to have each person count off. Choose a number from one to five, depending on the number of women in your group, by rolling a die or drawing from slips of paper with numbers written on them. Announce that the person with the chosen number is the designated facilitator of the Bible study.

Understand the Role of the Facilitator

The facilitator begins by reading the directions out loud to the group, unless the instructions state otherwise. It is helpful if each person has her own copy of the study. Read through all of the instructions before you begin the actual study. This is helpful to those who are visually oriented as well as to those who respond more easily to auditory instructions. It also gives everyone an overview the first time you use a new method.

The facilitator now goes back to the beginning of the printed instructions and guides the circle by reading each step again, this time pausing after each step so that everyone may follow the instructions. The facilitator does not add personal comments or rephrase the written text into her own words. She simply reads what is written. She also watches the time and indicates when the group should move on to the next step, which helps to keep the circle on schedule.

When it is time to share with one another, the facilitator does not call on participants but waits for individuals to volunteer. Anyone in the group may choose to pass by simply saying "pass." This decision should be respected.

✳ Four Methods of Sacred Story Bible Study

The four methods of Sacred Story Bible Study offered here are centered in matters that are divine. These spiritually centered methods provide an excellent tool for helping you and the women in your circle find spiritual nourishment in the midst of your busy lives. Not only may you use them when you meet as a circle, but you also may adapt them for use in a private devotional time at home. All of the methods include step-by-step directions, making them easy to use. Try each one to discover the methods that best suit the needs and personalities of you and your group. Alternating the four methods will lend variety to your circle's gatherings. (Note: These Sacred Story Bible Study methods also are featured in the resource *From the Heart Journal: A Personal Prayer Journal for Women*, which is a twelve-week spiritual growth program for women's groups.)

The four methods are (1) Praying the Scripture, (2) Awakening Hearts, (3) Imagining, and (4) Responsive Listening. Let's take a brief look at each method before moving on to a more detailed explanation of the steps involved.

1) Praying the Scripture is taken from the writings of Madame Guyon, a Christian woman who lived in France from 1648 to 1717. Her instructions on Scripture and prayer are as relevant today as they were over 280 years ago. Using this method, you read the Scripture together, journal your reflections, and then share your thoughts with one another.

2) Awakening Hearts includes reading the Scripture together and then journaling individually with a specifically stated focus.

3) Imagining invites you to close your eyes and place yourselves in the biblical scene as the Scripture is read.

4) Responsive Listening is an oral tradition Bible study that leads you in reading the Scripture together three times. After each reading, you pause to discern aloud God's will for your lives. (Note: This method of Bible study is used in the group resource *SpiritGifts: One Spirit, Many Gifts*.)

Sacred Story Method 1: Praying the Scripture

Read and hear the wise words of Madame Guyon. First, the facilitator reads the instructions to the group, which appear in bold print. She reads *only* the bold print. Then she goes back to the beginning and reads through the steps in their entirety, including Guyon's words, which appear in italics.

Step 1. *" 'Praying the Scripture' is a unique way of dealing with the Scripture; it involves both reading and prayer."* **Divide into small groups of three to**

five. Circle your chairs and sit knee to knee. Space the groups around the room.

Step 2. *"Turn to the Scripture; choose some passage that is simple and fairly practical. Next, come to the Lord. Come quietly and humbly."* **Turn to the selected Scripture text.**

Step 3. *"There, before him, read a small portion of the passage of Scripture you have opened to. Be careful as you read. Take in fully, gently, and carefully what you are reading. Taste it and digest it as you read. In the past it may have been your habit, while reading, to move very quickly from one verse of Scripture to another until you have read the whole passage. Perhaps you were seeking to find the main point of the passage."* **Reading out the passage slowly, with one person reading out loud. Take care that you read it fully and with gentleness.**

Step 4. *"But in coming to the Lord by means of 'praying the Scripture,' you do not read quickly; you read very slowly. You do not move from one passage to another, not until you have sensed the very heart of what you have read. You may then want to take that portion of Scripture that has touched you and turn it into prayer."* **Read the passage out loud in unison.**

Step 5. *"After you have sensed something of the passage, and after you know that the essence of that portion has been extracted and all the deeper sense of it is gone, then, very slowly, gently, and in a calmer manner begin to read the next portion of that passage. You will be surprised to find that when your time with the Lord has ended, you will have read very little, probably no more than half a page."* **Remain in silence. Begin to read the passage to yourself slowly and silently. Stop at the portion of Scripture that touches your heart. Write your reflections of this portion of Scripture that has drawn your attention. (Allow 2 minutes for writing.)**

Step 6. *" 'Praying the Scripture' is not judged by how much you read but by the way you read. If you read quickly, it will benefit you little. You will be like a bee that merely skims the surface of a flower. Instead, in this new way of reading with prayer, you become as the bee who penetrates into the depths of the flower. You plunge deeply within to remove its deepest nectar."* **Finally, take the portion of Scripture that stopped you and touched you and turn it into a simple sentence prayer of no more than ten to twelve words. Write your short prayer. Pray the prayer over and over in a calm manner. (Allow 3 minutes.)**

Step 7. *"Of course, there is a kind of reading the Scripture for scholarship and for study—but not here. That studious kind of reading will not help you when it comes to matters that are divine! To receive any deep, inward profit from the Scripture you must read as I have described. Plunge into the very depths of the words you read until revelation, like a sweet aroma, breaks out upon you. I am quite sure that if you will follow this course, little by little you will come to experience a very rich prayer that flows from your inward being."* **One at a time, share your prayer with the circle. You may choose to pass.**

Sacred Story Method 2: Awakening Hearts

In this method, you read the text, write your thoughts, and listen to others' reflections as you search your heart and discern what God is saying to you. It is important to remember that this is not a discussion group. Instead, the emphasis is on listening to and reflecting on the Scripture.

If you have not yet done so, divide into small circles of three to five. Choose women whom you know the least. Circle your chairs so that you are sitting knee to knee. Space the groups around the room.

One woman in each group serves as facilitator for the entire study. The facilitator reads the step-by-step directions aloud, stopping whenever a ♥ appears so that everyone in the group may respond. The three steps, used three times each, are **READ, WRITE**, and **TALK.** The circle then takes a fourth and final step: **PRAY.**

READ   One woman reads the Sacred Story aloud, slowly. ♥

WRITE   Reflect on this question: "What do I see, hear, and feel?" Write a brief response. We will pause for two minutes. ♥

TALK   Briefly share your response with the group without explanation. Listen to one another and do not comment on what others say. Receive each woman's offering as a gift. ♥

READ   Another woman reads the Sacred Story aloud, slowly, a second time. ♥

WRITE   How does the Sacred Story, and what others have shared, touch your heart? Complete the following in one sentence: "My heart is touched—" We will pause for two minutes. ♥

TALK   Briefly share your response. Others will not comment on what you share. They will serve as Christ's presence by listening and receiving until it is their turn. ♥

READ   Another woman reads the Sacred Story aloud, slowly, a third time. ♥

WRITE   As my heart is touched by all that I have heard, seen, and felt, what can I describe as God's wish for my life? Write one or two sentences. We will pause for two minutes. ♥

TALK   Share your responses using "I" statements. Share as time allows. Make sure to leave time for prayer. ♥

PRAY   One at a time, pray out loud for the woman on your right. Say the person's name and a brief prayer concerning what she shared. The circle may wish to join hands. ♥

You may talk quietly until all groups finish. ♥

Sacred Story Method 3: Imagining

In this Sacred Story Bible Study method, imagination is the point of contact between divine revelation and human experience. Imagination is a means of coming to a contemporary understanding of God and Scripture without violating traditional Christian understandings.

You will want to choose no more than ten to twelve verses for this method, unless the chosen story would be incomplete without adding additional verses. In this exercise, you read the Sacred Story three times. After each slow, thoughtful reading, close your eyes and use your imagination to discover the story's meaning for you.

One woman guides the entire process by reading each step, pausing whenever a ♥ appears so that everyone in the group may participate as directed. After reading each bulleted question, she will pause approximately thirty seconds. She may wish to use a watch or clock with a second hand.

If you have not yet done so, divide into small circles of three to five. Choose women whom you know the least. Circle your chairs so that you are sitting knee to knee. Space the groups around the room.

Step 1. One women reads the text aloud. ♥

Step 2. Close your eyes and use your imagination. Explore the scene fully. ♥ Now enter into the scene. ♥

I will read several questions. After reading each one, I will pause approximately thirty seconds.

- What is the setting? ♥
- What are the sounds, sights, and aromas? ♥
- Who else is there? ♥
- What do they look like? ♥
- What do their faces tell you? ♥

Step 3. Open your eyes and read the text out loud a second time. The same woman who read previously reads again. ♥

Step 4. Close your eyes and use your imagination. Again I will read several questions, pausing after each one for approximately thirty seconds.

- Where are you in the story? ♥
- What is your role in this drama? Let the story unfold. ♥
- Does anyone speak to you? ♥
- What does this person say? ♥
- What do you reply? ♥
- Is there other action of which you are a part? ♥
- What are you feeling? ♥

Step 5. Open your eyes. Read the text out loud a third time. The same woman again reads. ♥

Step 6. Now the story is concluded. Close your eyes and use your imagination. As before, I will read a few questions, pausing after each one for approximately thirty seconds.

- Do you go elsewhere? ♥

- Whom do you tell about what you just witnessed? ♥

Step 7. Bring your attention back to the present. Open your eyes. Consider this question silently for a moment.

- What questions or insights arise? ♥

Step 8. Now prepare to share with the circle.

- What is the story's meaning to you?

Share your responses with one another as time permits. ♥

Step 9. Close by praying God's will into your life. Share together this ecumenical text of the Lord's Prayer. Pray in the softness of a whisper. ♥

Our Father in heaven,
   hallowed be your name,
   your kingdom come,
   your will be done, on earth as in heaven.
Give us today our daily bread.
Forgive us our sins
   as we forgive those who sin against us.
Save us from the time of trial
   and deliver us from evil.
For the kingdom, the power, and the glory are yours
   now and for ever. Amen.
(*The United Methodist Hymnal.* Nashville: The United Methodist Publishing House, 1989, 894.)

Sacred Story Method 4: Responsive Listening

This Bible study approach helps us open ourselves to hear God's Word anew and apply it to our hearts and lives. Through the responsive listening method, Bible stories meet us in our own life stories. These stories allow us to gain insight and hear God's voice as we listen to what others have to share.

Through the lens of Scripture, you will be challenged to look at the present conditions of your life, your community, your nation, and your world. Together you will reflect on what the Bible is saying to you about your role in each story. Then you will be challenged to respond to one another and to take action grounded in prayer.

If you have not yet done so, divide into small circles of three to five. Choose women whom you know the least. Circle your chairs so that you are sitting knee to knee. Space the groups around the room.

Step 1. Read the passage slowly, with one person reading out loud. [3-4 minutes][2]

Step 2. In silence, recall the word, phrase, or sentence that most caught your attention and reflect on this. [1 minute]

Step 3. Each person shares the word, phrase, or sentence she chose with the circle without comment. [1-2 minutes]

Step 4. A different person reads the passage out loud again. [3-4 minutes]

Step 5. Think about: "Where does this passage touch my life (or our community, or our nation, or our world) today?" Each person responds using an "I" statement—not "The church thinks . . ." or "The world thinks . . .," but "I think . . ." [3-5 minutes]

---

2. These eight responsive listening steps are from *SpiritGifts: One Spirit, Many Gifts* by Patricia Brown © 1996 Abingdon Press. Used by permission.

Step 6. A different person reads the passage out loud again. [3-4 minutes]

Step 7. Think about: "From what I have heard and shared, what does God want me to do or be this week? How does God invite me to change?" Each person responds using an "I" statement. Share as time allows, making sure to leave time for prayer (step 8). You may want to jot down a word or two, but no more, as the person on your right is speaking, so that you will remember what to pray for in step 8. [3-5 minutes]

Step 8. One at a time, briefly pray out loud for the person on your right, naming what that person shared in step 7. The group may wish to join hands. [3-5 minutes]

Note: Be brief in steps 5 and 7. Do not elaborate, teach, or explain. Listen without responding. No one is to comment, critique, or build on what is said, as if in a discussion group. Talk quietly about what you just experienced until all of the groups are finished.

✳ Processing Sacred Story Bible Study

You and the other women in your circle will discover a great deal about yourselves through the dynamics of group process while engaging in the four methods of Sacred Story Bible Study. Many circles find it helpful to reflect on the group processes and dynamics involved in the methods before reading the remainder of this chapter. If you would like to do this, stop now. Then you may compare your notes to my following notes.

1. **"I" statements are important.** They force us to be mindful of the beam in our eye and to leave the mote in the other person's eye to God's care. This is not a narcissistic statement, but a statement that leads to accountability for the choices we make in our lives. Habit often leads us to use a general "we" when talking. The facilitator and/or participants in your group may want to remind one another to use "I" statements until everyone becomes accustomed to doing so.

2. **Some women may be preoccupied by thinking about what they want to say.** This may be especially true when first using a Sacred Story Bible Study approach. With time, you and the other women in your circle will learn to turn off your preoccupation with your own agendas and to "center in" on what others are saying.

3. **Women often feel the need to explain their statements.** We come from different backgrounds and cultures, and we need to be free to express our feelings in words that suit our meaning without the pressure to conform to some "norm." Many of us are fearful that our meaning may be misinterpreted. As the women in your circle learn to hear one another non-judgmentally, and trust develops, this defense will lessen.

4. **Women look for signs of acknowledgment and validation as they speak.** From the time we are little girls, we are conditioned to seek the confirmation of others—so much so, that we aren't even aware of the fact that our communication has been "taken over." We learn how to listen to others' comments and voice inflection and to watch their body language for clues to how we should respond. Bit by bit, we become self-referential, until one day we wake up as grown women who look outside rather than inside for direction. Yet when we invite one another to listen to ourselves, to speak our truths, and to be honored and supported in our search, we empower one another to trust ourselves enough to allow whatever "is" to simply emerge. We thus free ourselves from the need to seek approval.

In the book *Worshiping Women: Reforming God's People for Praise,* Heather Murray Elkins speaks about women's worship: "The final verdict of worthiness of any form of worship is not pronounced by a jury of our peers." What she has to say also may be applied to the open form of communication used in the Sacred Story Bible Study methods:. "Worthy? Who is worthy . . . and the roar of a thousand voices shouts down your doubt. . . . 'Worthy, yes, worthy! We are worthy!' " (Nashville: Abingdon Press, 1994, 20). God says we are already worthy as women who are baptized and chosen. It is unnecessary for us to seek our entire validation, approval, or even acknowledgment from another.

5. **Both the introvert and the extrovert find a safe space to share.** The first is not left out, and the second does not dominate.

6. **Some circle members have difficulty listening without speaking.** If you are one of these, you have to work at stifling the urge to jump in and comment on what others say. You will find, however, that you benefit most by sitting and observing your reactions. Ask yourself, "Isn't my reaction to what my circle friend is saying interesting?" Listening with our whole heart enables

us to extend our love to God and others. In this love we may be persons who are healthy, whole, and Christ-centered—persons with plenty to give others.

7. **Sacred Story Bible Study creates an intimacy that is authentic, not superficial.** Honesty breeds honesty. In my book *Learning to Lead from Your Spiritual Center,* I say it this way: "Outward and inward honesty are what we strive for as leaders. We commit to being transparent. We project to others none other than our authentic self. We do not have hidden parts of our lives that cannot be shown. There is not a secret life behind the persona we project. Another way to put it is, 'What you see is what you get' " (Nashville: Abingdon Press, 1996, 93).

8. **Women familiar with the Bible stories will hear them with a new ear.** Others, to whom the stories are new, will enjoy the inward searching and relational aspects of the study.

9. **Let silence be the rule, unless speaking will improve the silence.** Some women wrongfully believe, *If I'm not speaking, then nothing is happening.* Leave spaces for God to speak. Surprise, surprise—we may be able to hear

God's words to us through our sisters. Be comfortable with silences. Chapter 6 deals more with solitude.

✳ Choosing Scripture Texts

When choosing scriptures to use with any one of the four methods outlined in this chapter, you will want to limit the amount of text to approximately ten verses, give or take a few. More than this becomes overwhelming. Stories primarily from the Gospels are the best. The stories of Peter walking on the water, the prodigal son, and the feeding of the five thousand are all fine examples of texts that work well. Stories of Jesus' encounters with women are also quite effective. (Note: The women's group resource *Heart to Heart Guidebook: A Spiritual Journey for Women* draws upon the stories of Jesus' encounters with women.)

✳ Being Attentive to God's Word

Hear this wisdom drawn from *Heart to Heart Guidebook:* "When we read the Bible, we are reading the Word of God. When we listen carefully, the Word touches us in ways that move our hearts to live God's will. We are in rhythm with the heartbeat of God." "Being attentive to God means spending time with the Sacred Stories. When we listen carefully with our hearts as well as our heads, God's Word touches us in greater ways than we ever imagined possible" (132, 122).

As women, we want to be connected to the mystery of God. Our hungry hearts long for a mystical link to God, a link that is creative and life-giving. We seek encounters with God that feed the soul. Some of us do this intellectually; as we gain more knowledge, we come to know God. Others of us have a more intuitive approach to our relationship with God, taking into account our subjective experiences. For most of us, however, both the reasoning mind and the imaginative mind combine in our experience of God. The important thing is that God's spirit works individually with each one of us. As Mary Field Belenky and Nancy Rule Goldberger remind us with the title of their book, we are to respect *"women's ways of knowing."*

Perhaps some of us have had small revelatory experiences of God during a biblical reading. In our search for our hearts, we may have gained wisdom, solace, assurance, direction, and peace. Our experiences of God are real. We feel God's touch, hear God's voice, and sense God's presence. This allows us to be women full of God's creative, freeing Spirit.

As you read the Sacred Stories, *listen*—not only

with your head, but also with your heart, for God speaks both in the voice of reason and in the intuitive whisper of love. Amen! And Amen!

✳ Questions for Reflection and Action

1. Our goal in reading the Sacred Stories is to grow into a deeper, more authentic relationship with God—not simply to learn the contents of a biblical text. Which of the four methods would you like to try first? Why?

2. Which group dynamic of the nine discussed on pages 112-116 most caught your attention? Why?

3. Some women come to know God primarily by intellectually gaining knowledge of God. Other women strongly intuit their relationship with God, taking into account their subjective experiences. How do you experience God?

CHAPTER 6

Prayer Rituals

"Prayer is God's intimate conversation with your heart. Prayer is your heart-song—God's heart-song to you."

"My heart-song?" Questa repeats, listening with a new ear.

"God's Spirit within, touching your heart, knows things that your intellect does not," Sage explains. "Your heart-song—that which connects you to God, and God to you—sustains you through the trials of the journey. Prayer is God's care for you."

—The Quest of the Woman in Search of Her Heart

In my guest room hangs a friendship quilt created out of odds and ends of colorful cloth. It is lovingly embroidered with the names of women. The quilt was made by members of a small church in the Endless Mountains of Pennsylvania and presented to me, their first woman pastor. In this rural setting, quilting remains an opportunity for women to gather and ritualize together. Images such as weaving and quilting often find their way into women's ritual, calling to mind the complex interconnectedness that patterns women's lives. Women create spiritual practices unique to them that draw upon their own strengths.

Many collective activities and gatherings of women are ritualized. Sweet sixteen birthday parties and baby and wedding showers are ritualized rites of passage into new stages of womanhood. Attending garden clubs, "doing lunch," and working in the kitchen to prepare a meal are all notable instances of women's ritualizing.

✳ Prayer and Your Spirituality Circle

It is important that prayer rituals be a part of every circle meeting. The word says it all: you are a women's spirituality circle. Spirit *rituals*, or what circles call "prayer rituals," carry deeper meanings in their words or actions than what may first appear.

In her book *Ritualizing Women,* Lesley A. Northup lifts up the common traits in women's ritual. She addresses women's rituals of many faith traditions. For our purposes, I list six traits and comment on them from a Christian perspective.

1. Women's prayer rituals are creative.

Women's prayer rituals are creative, dynamic, spontaneous, and responsive to the needs of the circle. They reflect the talents and interests of the participants even as they respond to current events and shared concerns. As such, prayer rituals become a sustaining force within the community, especially when women use practices that are adaptable and resourceful.

Your prayer rituals may be serious or silly, solemn or playful, depending on the needs and mood of your group. The actual end process of the ritual is not as important as the process itself; the process supersedes the product. Although rituals may be repeated and built upon, you'll want to be careful not to turn rituals into rites, which become frozen and unmoving.

Even established rituals with biblically mandated texts and a rich tradition are personalized by women. For example, the Eucharist, sometimes called the Lord's Supper or Holy Communion, may be personalized. Those who personalize rituals emphasize the performative action, informality, and spontaneity even as we uphold the theological integrity of the written text, actions, and form.

Sue, pastor of a small worshiping community in the midst of a large membership church, shares Communion weekly with those who attend a coffeehouse style gathering. Sue understands that the presence of Christ is to be at the center of the service, not any devotional talk that she might share or song the musicians play. She recites from heart the words of the Prayer of Great Thanksgiving and, in a gentle manner, teaches the history and meaning of the ritual actions: "Third-century Christians shared these same words of celebration. They too gathered to break bread and recall the salvation story. . . . The confession and peace are a time for us to examine our lives and turn our hearts in love to both God and our neighbor. . . . The single cup shows our unity." Participants come forward to receive, enriched in their new insights into the mysteries of the faith.

In other instances, women often create inventive ritual rather than observing or participating in a fixed, received ritual. We use our own words, diverting from something that is printed. Enacted prayer rituals and actions are usually simultaneously or sequentially communal.

Pastor Debbie invited the children to gather around the baptismal fountain as she observed the printed ritual of the book of worship. After the squirming baby girl had received the formal rite, Debbie veered from the stayed ritual and told the children that they too could dip their fingers into the pool of water. Each child excitedly placed the water upon her or his head and recited this line as they returned to their seats: "I remember my baptism and am thankful."

2. In women's prayer rituals, the domestic is sacred.

The main function of much religious ritual is to move the believer out of the temporal into a sacred reality. Women's ritual does this, but it also is clearly rooted in the here and now. Prayer rituals offer a spiritual expression of the ordinary domesticity of women's lives. Therefore, women's rituals are often grounded in the lives, work, and activities of women: housework, cooking, parenting, dressing, managing, networking, teaching—an endless host of women's unglorified daily tasks.

3. Women's prayer rituals highlight sensory experiences.

When women do prayer rituals, we tend to explore a state of being, favoring a vision of God's indwelling divinity or power. Prayer rituals provide a way for us to get more deeply in touch with God and with our sense of self.

Some of us may have been taught that laughter is not acceptable in the church arena, although crying is permitted. We have been trained to enter into religious actions with somber inner control. Women's prayer rituals give us an outlet for emotional expressions with an emphasis on our sensory experiences: our feelings, needs, and yearnings.

As women, we tend to be more playful in the midst of rituals. We are willing to laugh and let it feel good. For some of us, after years of suppression, it is wonderful to allow our feminine spirit to rise again. We amaze even ourselves to find that laughter is not hostile to spirituality, and that play can have profound power.

4. Women's ritual centers on connection and relationship.

Women's acts of ritual lift up interconnection rather than individualism. Relationship, rather than hierarchy, is a key organizational principle in women's groups. Developing a creed or a written code of conduct is not a priority, whereas sharing common values and a tolerance of diversity are extremely important. Perhaps this is why women's prayer rituals usually happen in the margins and often are not institutionally used in the larger church community.

5. Prayer ritual moves women to justice.

Prayer ritual gets us moving. It focuses on movement rather than stasis; on vocalization rather than passive listening. Through prayer ritual, we discover the wellsprings of God's Spirit that gush up with immense vitality and energy. It is not surprising, then, that the convictions expressed in the rituals often lead us beyond religious meaning into concerns for justice and inspire us to work for change. When we pray, we are time and again met with the challenge to transform society, even as Christ transforms our hearts from the inside out.

Praying gives us a sense of being a participant rather than a pawn in life's drama. We leave the circle meeting with a greater commitment to Christ. We work at the thrift shop, tutor children, go the extra mile at work, and really listen to our children. My own mother was moved to care for children orphaned by war in Rwanda and Zaire. Partaking in a ritual is symbolic action that has the power to effect change because one's view of reality is altered.

6. Prayer rituals offer Christ-centered identity.

Many woman who enter into spirituality circles are looking for a powerful new community—a community of Spirit-minded, Christ-centered women who are seeking ways to express their faith through symbols and metaphors that affirm their own experiences as daughters of God. Ritual has the ability to draw women together, to communicate values and goals, and to forge the group into a united Christian community. Prayerful rituals provide a platform for both identity and community.

✴ Seasonal Prayer Rituals to Plan and Use

Here are eight prayer rituals that may be used during various times of the Christian calendar and that fit with specific biblical stories.

1. They Will Call Me Blessed — *Christmas Season* (Mary's Song of Praise, Luke 1:26-56) Bread is an important symbol in the Christian faith. Use a sweet bread for this prayer ritual. Place the bread in the middle of the focus center. As you tear off a piece of the bread and offer it to any sister in the circle, say to her, "He has filled the hungry with good things" (Luke 1:53). Later, as you prepare to leave, one at a time take the hand of the woman beside you and say the angel's message to Mary: "You are blessed." After each woman has been blessed, in unison say, "Amen!"

2. New Light — *Season of Epiphany* (The Woman Who Touched Jesus, Mark 5:25-34) On the focus center, place a white candle. Surround the candle with smaller candles of different colors, one for each woman. Each woman may decide for herself what her light means to her. Invite the women to light their candles as they name the new wisdom they received in the past year. After each woman has shared her new discovery, light the white candle and sing a song of praise to Christ. Allow the women to take their lights with them into the world.

3. Bowl of Tears — *Season of Lent* (A Near Death Experience, John 7:53–8:11) In a time of silence, invite each woman to write down a regret on a slip of paper: a fight with a loved one, a road not taken, or a harsh word said in anger. Then pass a ceremonial bowl around the circle and invite each person to place into it her regret. Place the bowl in the middle of the focus center. Have each woman dip her fingers into a "Blessing Bowl" full of water and sprinkle symbolic tears over the slips of paper. As each woman sprinkles the tears, she says, "In the name of Jesus, I am forgiven."

4. Healing Our Hurts — *Easter Season* (The Woman Who Anointed Jesus, Mark 14:3-9) The root of the word *healing* in the New Testament Greek means "make whole." We can become channels of God's love as we pray for the healing that comes from God.

Give a piece of white ribbon to each woman. Read aloud the following: "The white ribbon represents the wounds we carry. As I take the white ribbon, I covenant with God and my sisters here to work and pray for the healing of all persons, especially women who have been abused and battered. I join them in solidarity and commit myself to end suffering wherever it occurs: in our workplaces, in our churches, and in our homes." Each participant then asks her neighbor to tie the ribbon around her wrist. The women wear their white ribbons as an Easter witness to the healing of God's love.

5. Claiming the Spirit — *Season of Pentecost* (The Coming of the Holy Spirit, Acts 2:17-18) As a simple closing ritual, pass around a basket filled with deflated red, yellow, and orange balloons. The Hebrew word *ruah* means "breath." It is the breath of God that gives us life. Invite each woman to take a balloon and blow into it the breath of the Holy Spirit. Tie the balloons and bounce them overhead, passing them to one another. Watch the flames of the Spirit dance upon your heads. Anyone passing by will think you've been filled with new wine! Close with a simple prayer of thanksgiving. Say in unison, "Thank you, Holy Spirit, for your breath that lives within us. Amen!"

6. Waiting to Exhale — *The Season of Advent* (The Bent-Over Woman, Luke 13:10-17) This is a fun one. Collect the following props and set them on the focus center: a red hat, a pair of white gloves, a jar of pickles, a stick, slippers, a plastic flower, pens and pencils in a box, a newspaper. Entice one woman to be the actor for the group and have her take center stage. As the volunteer playfully enacts the drama, the remainder of the circle reads the poem "Warning" by Jenny Joseph, also known by the title "When I Am an Old Woman I Shall Wear Purple" (Sandra Martz, ed. *When I Am an Old Woman I Shall Wear Purple*. Watsonville, Calif.: Papier-Mache Press, 1991, 1). Most groups have at least one ham, and this is her moment to shine.

7. Tongsung Kido — *Any Season* (Praying Aloud, Romans 8:26) *"Likewise the Spirit helps us with our weakness; for we do not know how to pray as we ought, but that very Spirit intercedes with sighs too deep for words."*

The United Methodist Book of Worship describes this group prayer:

> In Korean congregations, . . . Tongsung Kido is popular and an important part of prayer life. Usually the congregation is given a specific time period, with a common theme
> . . . Then all pray aloud at the same time. The voices of others will not bother them when they concentrate on their own earnest prayers, longing for the empowerment of the Holy Spirit (Nashville: The United Methodist Publishing House, 1992, 445).

Turn and kneel at your seat, using your chair as a prayer altar. Then invite the circle to pray out loud their needs and concerns at the same time, allowing five to ten minutes. Give a signal when time is up, perhaps with the use of a bell. To close, pray the Lord's Prayer in a loud voice, with arms raised.

8. Body Prayer — *Any Season* (1 Corinthians 6:19-20) *"Therefore glorify God in your body"* (1 Corinthians 6:20) From what we know about body language, outward posture often is indicative of our inward state. The body, mind, and spirit cannot be separated. This prayer is called "Palms Up, Palms Down."

Begin by placing your palms down to symbolize your desire to relinquish to God all your concerns. Let go. Practice this release for two minutes.

Now, turn your palms up to symbolize your desire and openness to receive from the Lord. Identify before God what you need for two minutes.

Spend the next two minutes in silence. Be still in your heart and sit in God's presence. Let the Lord speak to you.

✳ Jump In and Do It!

Debating endless hours about how to do a prayer ritual or discussing its deeper meaning is not always necessary. I often find it is best to jump right in and do prayer. See how prayer works and feels. It is not always true that ritual must represent something. Sometimes reality works the other way; the meaning develops out of the doing.

A prayer ritual can have many layers of meaning for different women, and each woman relates in her own way. Some ways of being in the presence of God work for some individuals and groups but not for others. Because prayer affects different people in different ways, you'll want to have a time to debrief afterward. Talk about it and share what happened.

✳ A Word About Fasting from Speech

At times in your prayer rituals, your circle will choose to "fast from speech." For five or ten minutes, or whatever time is allotted, you abstain from speaking to one another. This means that you stop all talk from the moment the time begins until you return as a full group, breaking the silence together.

If your circle is not used to solitude, these minutes may seem like a lifetime. Yet it is good to take time from our hectic lives to stop. The spiritual work of solitude is as important as any task or project your circle will undertake. Do not feel guilty about slowing down and "wasting time." Persons don't

—— 131 ——

constantly have to be "on stage." It is permissible to care for your own soul. Spending time with God on the spiritual journey is essential work.

Here's how it works. Invite each member of your circle to find a quiet space to claim as her own. You may want to move to a different part of the room, another room, or outside. A facilitator lets everyone know when time is up. A whispered invitation to each woman or a soft bell will do the trick. The circle then may reconvene and break your period of silence with prayer or music.

Learning comes as you observe your feelings and reactions. Become aware of what you are feeling in this time spent in solitude, in this time apart. When you follow God's command to love your neighbor as yourself, you take time to know yourself, this person you are to love. Ask yourself: What does this experience tell me about myself? This is not a selfish love; it is genuine care for your own spiritual well-being that enables you to give and to be fully present to others.

In addition to times during prayer rituals, you also may choose to fast from speech as you open the circle gathering. Take five minutes to sit and literally catch your breath. Use this time for an "attitude adjustment." This creates a space for individuals to center and quiet themselves in God's and in one another's presence. It also tends to focus the group and settle everyone down. Women begin to be aware of other people and of their own inner feelings. Fasting from speech also can help focus the circle when it is time to write in your journals as a group activity. It is a time of solitude to search out your own heartsongs.

There are few promises in this book, but I do promise you that you will not grow spiritually if you do not take regular time-outs for prayerful, reflective, meditative solitude. Silence means not only the absence of speech but also a new openness to listen. To stop talking, without listening to God, is not true spiritual solitude. The constant talker drains her inner energy without realizing it. In silence she learns that she can turn off the stream of talk and still feel at ease with others. In the quiet she also learns to listen to her sisters. As she silences herself, she grows increasingly sensitive and gentle toward others. When she learns to listen and be still, she is able to speak the word of compassion that is needed when it is needed. With practice, your circle may find that you like the discipline of silence as much as talking.

Women in circles that practice inner silence begin to learn the lessons of maintaining a quiet place of mind and heart *at all times*—a quiet place designed for silence and solitude. This time of fasting ripples out to the other parts of their lives.

Women begin to anticipate the snatches of quiet times here and there throughout their day—in the morning before the kids get up, or later in the day while sitting in the car at a red light. They stop for a minute of silence before they eat. Bit by bit, they learn to carry a portable sanctuary of the heart wherever they go.

✳ Questions for Reflection and Action

1. What prayer rituals will you create for your circle? Create ten prayer rituals to use as openings and closings of circle gatherings.

2. When do you fast from speech? Make a list of times in your daily schedule when you will begin to intentionally observe times of silence and reflection.

3. Sue and Debbie show us examples of ritual that are communal, spontaneous, and informal even as they enrich the traditions of the Christian faith. What examples can you give?

CHAPTER 7

Be-Attitudes for Circles

Perhaps you are looking in the wrong places to find your heart. The heart's deepest lessons are often where you least expect to find them. And sometimes the ways are hard.
       —The Quest of the Woman in Search of Her Heart

The Beatitudes of Jesus found in the Gospel of Matthew are not a set of rules for living or a ladder to moral success. Instead, they are a description of what it is like to live and to see life from within the commonwealth of God. Here are some "Be-Attitudes" for women's spirituality groups that will help give an understanding of your community life together. Some are short and to the point. Others take some time to explain. Enjoy.

• **Be-gin and end on time.** Thirty-minute gatherings should end in thirty minutes. Sixty-minute gatherings should end in sixty minutes. Many women have childcare or elder care responsibilities, and many will sandwich this time for themselves in between a child's ball game and a dental appointment. If people know you begin and end at the designated times, they will plan their schedules accordingly. Be respectful and value your and others' precious time.

• **Be trustworthy.** Respect each woman's thoughts, feelings, and beliefs based on her life experiences and knowledge. Trust that others will respect you. This means you do not talk about each other outside of the group, even among yourselves. If you have something to say about someone, say it to her face or not at all.

Stay away from any kind of gossip during or after the meetings. We've all had the experience of hearing from a third party something negative someone has said about us. It leaves a terrible feeling in the pit in your stomach, and it doesn't give you kind feelings toward the other person. If you find the need to discuss someone, make it a hard and fast rule to pray for the person before and especially after the discussion.

• **Be committed to creating a community of the Spirit.** Sacred Scripture says, "In [Christ Jesus] the whole structure is joined together and grows into a holy temple in the Lord; in whom you also are *built together spiritually into a dwelling place for God*" (Ephesians 2:21-22, italics added). Intentionally remain focused on your core purpose of spiritual formation. Continually ask the hard questions that will keep your circle centered on your relationship with God.

Of course, members will miss meetings occasionally. Family and work needs arise, women get overwhelmed, and calendars get overloaded. Have grace for one another in these times, trusting that each woman is where she needs to be. Also be conscious, however, of the choice you have made to be part of this circle. Put the date on your calendar and keep it for your own spiritual nourishment.

• **Be accepting of each person.** Live in nonjudgment. Know that we seek God in different ways. As we noted in chapter 5, some of us do this intellectually; as we gain more knowledge, we come to know God. Others of us have a more intuitive approach to our relationship with God, taking into account our subjective experiences. God's Spirit works individually with each one of us. You may know God through thinking, while the woman sitting across the room from you may know God through feeling. The intellectual is not considered superior to the emotional. For most of us, the reasoning mind and the imaginative mind combine in our experience of God. When we listen carefully with our hearts as well as with our heads, God's Word touches us in greater ways than we ever imagined possible. Respect different ways of knowing.

- **Be an attentive listener.** Listen without interrupting. When someone in the circle is sharing, listen without talking or whispering to your neighbor. Take turns speaking, one at a time, while others listen.

  You will learn a great deal about yourselves within the interchanges of group process. At first, you may be preoccupied with thinking about what you want to say. While you are listening, don't worry about your turn. Instead, be 100 percent present for the person who is talking. Over time, you will learn to turn off your preoccupation with your own agenda and center in on what others say. Trust yourself enough to allow what you want to say to emerge. You don't have to articulate every idea perfectly. We're all "in process."

- **Be one who engengers confidence.** What about privacy issues? I recommend a hard and fast rule: Never say hurtful things behind someone's back. Keep confidential information to yourself. As trust grows, each of you will be open to experience the discomfort of both giving and receiving honest, constructive feedback. You may want to begin your sessions, as one group does, by going around the circle and each sharing a word of gratitude—a gift, kindness, or thanksgiving you experienced that week. Then raise the risk level by going around a second time and sharing what you each want to invite into your life. If any of you are keeping prayer journals, you may share with the circle only as you choose. Otherwise, your writings are private and confidential.

• **Be a supportive and affirming presence.** Do not preach, give advice, problem solve, make interpretations, or try to rescue others. Someone may disagree with this approach, saying that she feels odd not responding to the speaker immediately in a verbal way. Nevertheless, commit to giving one another the space to be your true selves. As each of you gains clarity, you will learn to solve your own problems. This means listening without an agenda.

When we listen with preconceived notions, we are busy trying to mold the person into the idea of who we think she should be. We are asking, "Does this person see things the right way—my way?" Upon this question we unwittingly place our approval or disapproval. It is not of primary importance if you agree or disagree with another in the circle. It is not a matter of someone being right and someone else being wrong. What is of central importance is that you are fully present with the person who is speaking. Understand how she feels and where she is coming from. Period.

Attentive listening provides the support and encouragement necessary to help us move out of our self-protective armor and fear of judgment. We can express our feelings without the pressure to conform to a norm. As we attend to one another's conversation in nonjudgmental ways, the speaker is free to name her reality and to hear God's truth for her life.

• **Be gentle-hearted with yourself and others.** Give yourself permission to talk or to pass. Share in the role of leadership as the opportunity comes to you and as you are able. Many of us don't have compassion for ourselves or acceptance of our true selves. It is an illusion to think we have compassion for others when we don't have it for ourselves. Don't be fooled. We cannot care for others when we have little, if any, forgiveness for our own humanness.

As previously mentioned, a hard and fast rule is never to speak harmful things behind a sister's back. Instead, focus on the common threads of sisterhood and support one another.

• **Be a consensus builder.** Circle decisions are made collectively. Problems are solved primarily through consensus. On some days, your circle may decide to get down to some serious work. On other occasions, you may choose to step away from the agenda to respond to an individual's pressing needs, to celebrate one another, or to watch a favorite episode of *I Love Lucy!*

How are decisions made? The answer is by alignment. You decide together by weighing in on the matter at hand. There is no vote. As you talk things over, the circle eventually pulls together.

• **Be open to share from your true self.** Use first person language (I, me, myself) when speaking. Habit often leads us to use a general "we" when talking. You may need to remind one another to use "I" statements until everyone grows accustomed to doing so. Although it is not the norm, claiming your experience as yours is important. Don't generalize about how "they" feel or what "everyone" thinks. This important "I" statement leads us to accountability for the choices we make in our lives. Say what you think and how you feel *specifically.*

• **Be honest.** Personal authenticity and genuine community are central. When we stop using our energy to look good or acceptable to others, to be right, or to appear perfect, we can wholeheartedly put our vitality into being real and whole. We grow tired of pseudocommunity and want the real thing. Women's spirituality circles create an intimacy that is authentic, not superficial. Integrity breeds integrity.

• **Be comfortable with silences.** One community of Christian monks lives in the understanding that silence is the rule unless speaking will improve the silence. What a refreshing notion to the usual chatter we experience in groups. Some wrongfully believe, "If I'm not speaking, then nothing is happening." Silence is truly golden, because it is so rare.

And finally . . .

• **Be responsible for your own needs.** Don't blame others for your feelings of anger or hurt. No one is responsible for your feelings but you.

Ask for what you need. Don't expect people to read your mind and respond appropriately. There may be intuitive individuals in your circle, but chances are good that they are not mind readers.

Each of you should be comfortable enough to share only as you choose. If any of you directly tells the group that you do not wish to share or to lead at a particular time, that should be accepted without question. It is perfectly acceptable to decline participation in a discussion or prayer ritual when you feel the need to be quiet or for any reason. The rest of the group, however, does not have to change to accommodate you. The important thing to keep in mind is not to expect the circle to intuit and respond "all-knowingly."

Come to think of it, these are good Be-Attitudes for life in general!

✳ Questions for Reflection and Action

1. Which Be-Attitude do you consider vital to the well-being of the circle? Which are essential for your personal well-being?

2. How have you felt when someone has violated one of the Be-Attitudes in a group you have participated in? Practice using an "I" statement to express your feelings.

3. How do you know when someone is present with you 100 percent? What are the outward signs of a good listener? What skills do you need to put in place in order to be a good listener?

CHAPTER 8

Will the Circle Be Unbroken?

If you truly want to know yourself, then you must live side-by-side with those whose opinions, needs, and lifestyles clash with your own. If you remain here and shelter yourself from the give-and-take of relationships, you can maintain the illusion of how "nice" you are. But as you dare to move out into the world, you will confront in yourself what you must overcome in order to take the next step to finding your heart.

—The Quest of the Woman in Search of Her Heart

❋ How Do You Keep Your Circle Healthy?

Your circle is together not because you see everything the same way. Nor because you are always comfortable with one another. The truth is that you gather, not to make a safe and exclusive place for yourselves, but to create a community of women who can begin to picture a different way of living. You are together because this is where God calls you to be—in community. The mystery of God's community is that God includes all people, no matter what their differences. God invites you to be sisters to one another.

This means that differences will probably arise, making it necessary for your group to set aside times for assessment. Because groups shift and change over time as they develop their own unique personalities, I recommend that your circle revisit your focus at least once a year. This assures that everyone is still walking in the same direction.

✻ Asking the Hard Questions

I recommend that ongoing circles intentionally set aside times to ask the hard questions and to make any needed course corrections. Like any healthy community, circles need to step back from time to time and take stock. It is good to regularly engage in self-reflection to raise fundamental questions: Are we growing in our relationship with God and with one another? Does our original intention and commitment remain clear? Are we having fun?

Remember that your focus is to foster Christ-centered spiritual formation in *all* the members of your circle. This intent is the measuring stick by which you assess the group. Are the women in your circle gaining a deeper, broader sense of who they are in relationship with God, their neighbor, and themselves? Are members open to the movement of God's Spirit in their lives?

Of course, the outward signs of such change vary

in different women. Barbara has returned to school and is taking classes at the local community college. Arlene is making a concerted effort not to repeat the past by being drawn into unhealthy relationships. Sue left a church position that had become more of a burden than a challenge. The evidence looks different, yet has much in common: overcoming self-doubt and becoming empowered—gaining hope and freedom.

✳ Two Avenues of Assessment

There are two ways this necessary monitoring may take place. One is the ongoing, spontaneous feedback of individuals which naturally occurs each time you meet. If a concern arises, take responsibility to speak up and name it. You probably aren't the only one who noticed or who has the same concern. Because we have been socially conditioned to be nice, sometimes we are unwilling to talk about seemingly small stuff. Instead of shoving our feelings down inside us, we can make the corrections and adjustments necessary as the group goes along.

A second way to monitor yourselves is to schedule group reviews at regular intervals for self-assessment and improvement. This more comprehensive type of reflection can be vital to group health. One circle who operates on a six-week cycle regularly re-examines themselves to see if they are going in the right direction or if they want to change course.

For long-term, ongoing groups, I suggest you set aside time at least once a year for self-assessment. If your circle meets weekly, for example, you might go on a two-day retreat each year to assess your progress and to plan for the coming year. Here is a list of helpful questions that may give you some insight. Begin by choosing two or three.

1. What have you appreciated most about the circle?

2. How has participating in the group changed your life?

3. Do you have needs that are not being met by the group? If so, what are they?

4. If you could change one thing about the circle, what would it be?

5. Are there cliques within the group? If so, how does that feel to you?

6. How is each person contributing to the task of

leadership? Are there individuals who overwork for the group?

7. What direction would you like to see the circle take in the next six weeks? In the coming months? In the next year? What changes do you hope for?

A second option is to use a written response form, such as the one that follows, so that participants may reflect on the questions and write responses before coming to the assessment meeting. The forms may be mailed to members or distributed at the meeting before the assessment process.

CIRCLE ASSESSMENT QUESTIONNAIRE

This assessment of your experience is important to the circle. It will help us to focus on how we are operating and to make any needed adjustments.

Rate each aspect of the experience as follows: 4—superb, 3—very good, 2—so-so, 1—not for me, 0—doesn't apply.

Prayer Rituals

Focus Center

Friendship and Support

Personal Prayer Journal

Relaxation Breathing

Symbolic Articles

Prayers and Poems

Sacred Story Bible Studies

Other:

The most helpful aspect of the circle for me personally has been:

The least helpful aspect of the circle for me personally has been:

Did this experience affect your spiritual life? If so, how?

Did this experience affect your personal or work life? If so, how?

If you could change one thing about how the circle operates, what would it be?

✱ Practical Advice to Keep Your Circle Healthy

Just because you are a women's Christian spirituality group does not guarantee that everything will be sweetness and light. Be careful not to idealize or romanticize your circle. Remember that you are human creatures, full of both conflict and brokenness as well as hope and courage. This "working out our salvation with fear and trembling" can be a very messy business. Spirituality doesn't mean that everyone lives happily ever after. Here is some practical advice for keeping your circle healthy throughout its lifetime.

1. Keep focused on your intended purpose of spiritual formation, and don't get sidetracked by frequently beginning late or succumbing to chitchat that leads the group away from your focus. Those who want to catch up with each other can plan to arrive early or to remain late.

2. If you are spending an inordinate amount of time on one person's issues, make sure you are not leaning too far in the direction of acting as a therapy or support group.

3. A woman who repeatedly fails to attend may be signaling that there is a problem within the group that needs to be addressed. This is a wonderful opportunity, not to focus on one individual's supposed failure ("What's wrong with her?") but to look deeper into the group's workings. What is missing that is essential to the well-being of the whole group? See this as an opportunity for the group to grow in its sense of Christian community. Keep in mind that the person who has missed frequently may not even realize the inner concerns that are being brought to light.

4. Problems emerge when power becomes unbalanced. This may not be overt power of one person over another. Instead, it can be very low key, such as when one member manipulates the conversation or when an introvert gives way to the more vocal extroverted voice. It takes consciousness to maintain a balance of power within a group. Work on establishing a broad balance of

group empowerment so that all women have ownership.

5. Expect subtle forces of resistance as women's Christian spirituality groups become powerful agents through which the Holy Spirit can transform the church. Our strength and empowerment is frightening to some.

   Watch out for divide-and-conquer tactics from the outside. Resist the inclination to renounce your sisters when you sense this tactic being employed. For example, people may talk about "those women," causing you to keep a safe distance from other women so that you will not be branded. Instead, focus on unity.

6. Name and deal with conflicts as they arise. Remember that conflict can be helpful and needs to be respected (and *expected*). Don't end conflict by smoothing over the difficulty. Listen and ask clarifying questions. Agree to think and pray about differences. This will open the group to new ways in which God may be speaking.

7. Watch out for triangulation. Triangulation is when one person talks to a third person

instead of talking directly to the person with whom she has a conflict. Address the conflict directly with the person involved. Learning to recognize and deal with conflict in your circle is great practice for life.

8. Celebrate and remember the lighter side of life. Be renewed in the joy of one another's company. The subtleties of women's humor is difficult to pinpoint but is vital to the health of the group. Laugh, dance, or sing a silly song. Remember to share your small victories and most humbling moments with one another.

   How do you do this and still "keep faith" with your circle's focus and time allowance? In one closing prayer ritual in the resource *Heart to Heart Guidebook: A Spiritual Journey for Women*, the participants are invited to throw pixy dust in all directions to remind themselves to take life lightly. Although this may seem silly to an outsider looking in, those who understand the greater significance see it as pure, unadulterated fun.

✳ A Labor of Love

Creating a circle and keeping it together in healthy ways is a labor of love. Because your group is like a living organism, it will require patience, compassion, and at times, the willingness to "run naked." We must be willing to risk and to step away from the old idea that being spiritual means being perfect. Instead, *spiritual* means truth-telling, vulnerability, and a willingness to take on the uncomfortable.

When we speak of a spiritual person, we aren't speaking of the dour church lady, who is pious beyond reproach. Instead, we envision a woman who is alive in the Spirit, exciting to be with, and creatively living each moment to the maximum. She is a guest you would want to invite to your next New Year's Eve party!

So, hold on to your seats and get ready for the ride. Let the party begin!

✳ Questions for Reflection and Action

1. Which questions will you ask in your assessment? Circle the ones you think would be most helpful to your particular group. Now create an assessment tool using those questions.

2. Which one of the eight advisory statements (pages 150-153) do you feel is most important to keeping your circle healthy?

3. Envision yourself as a "spiritual person." What do you look like? How do you act?

CHAPTER 9

Resources for Your Circle

Finding and listening to my heart,
finding out who I am
and who God is,
have not been simple.
It took time for the chatter to quiet down;
but then, in the silence of "not doing,"
in simply "being,"
I began to know what I felt.
Even now, if I listen really hard
and hear what is offered,
the Spirit is my guide.
  —The Quest of the Woman in Search of Her Heart

Circles that are faithful will engage us at the point of our deepest needs and desires, speak to us of faith, help us wrestle with questions and answers, and then send us out as ministers to our communities. Wendy M. Wright speaks of this reality with eloquence:

The sharing we do in the church, the body of Christ, is more than fellowship, more than working side by side. We share in a profound communion at the root of our beings. . . . We are lives interconnected at the core. Flowing from the same spring, the waters of divine life pulse through each of our beings, joining us as tributaries angling off from a single waterway.

We are mothers to one another, carrying each other beneath our hearts, slinging one another high on waiting hips when the walking becomes too difficult, lifting our hands behind each others' necks to bring hungry mouths to feed, giving our own substance to bring each other life. (*The Rising: Living the Mysteries of Lent, Easter, and Pentecost.* Nashville: Upper Room Books, 1994, 88-89)

Circles are interested in resources that will help them form and be transformed. Therefore, the rhythm of your circle gathering must be orchestrated with care. As you begin planning, ask yourselves what you hope to achieve. Then find the elements that interplay to create a flowing instrument for spiritual growth. There are powerful tools at your fingertips to magnify the message you want to convey. Your opening prayer ritual prepares women for what is to come. Similarly, your closing ritual identifies what you want the women to carry with them as they leave. Select music, readings, stories, Scriptures, reflection questions, symbols, and movement that create the mood you hope to elicit. Balance sound and silence, reflection and sharing, contemplation and action.

This final chapter presents an overview of the various resources you will need for your circle gatherings, complete with specific suggestions and even a few ready-to-use samples to help get you started. Feel free to depart from these ideas and suggestions and do your own thing to meet the unique needs and interests of your group. Have fun!

✳ Music to Inspire

Inspirational music provides a soulful gateway to spiritual feelings and ideas. Its influence is immediate, nonverbal, and more directly absorbed than complex systems of belief. The power of music is a gift that brings together the sacred and the sensual. It connects the earthly and the divine. Music carries us beyond the everyday to envision something greater than ourselves.

During your circle gatherings, use soothing meditative music as a respite from the hectic pace of ordinary life. Gentle music playing in the background makes people feel "at home," helps women ease into silences, and covers up disturbing sounds. When choosing music for times of silent reflection, stay away from familiar songs that might distract participants' thoughts during times of meditation. Other circle rituals will call for music that invites stirring, energized movement.

Don't be afraid to be creative in your selection of music. Music from Greek Byzantine chants, France's Taizé, Irish melodies, Trappist monks, American spirituals, and Spanish medieval cantigas are all rich sacred resources available to you. If you like, go multicultural and indulge in Jewish songs, Tibetan chanting and drumming, and West African ceremonial dance rhythms. Call me traditional (my tradition), but I enjoy the more sublime. Here are some of my picks:

ABoneCroneDrone, Sheila Chandra. Beautiful music for moments of inspiration and insight. You'll appreciate the multicultural pieces.

The Book of Secrets, Loreena McKennitt. Soothing Celtic music for the soul. Though this is my personal favorite, anything she has recorded is wonderful.

Hildegard Von Bingen (1098–1179), Anonymous 4. You'll be enchanted by Hildegard's miraculous, mystical music as chanted and performed by the Anonymous 4.

Migration, Peter Kater and Carlos Nakai. Great for prayer and meditation. With selections such as "Initiation," "Surrender," and "Transformation," this music will lead you to recognize the sacred in your life.

New Beginning, Tracy Chapman. "I'm Ready,"

and "New Beginning" are both jazzy selections that hit me where I live.

A Place in the World, Mary Chapin Carpenter. Whether or not you are a country music lover, you'll appreciate her powerful lyrics.

Shepherd Moon, Enya. Relaxing, with a Celtic twist. Any of Enya's CDs are great, but this one is my favorite. She is a woman who, by mixing her music in a recording studio, does it all!

Songs and Prayers from Taizé, the French Christian youth movement. The music and the accompanying book are both beautifully done. You'll fall in love with their chants of praise. Sing along with the tranquil, repeated refrains.

Walela, Rita Coolidge, Laura Satterfield, Priscilla Coolidge. This sassy recording brings a modern accent to Southwestern music. You'll love dancing around the living room to "Wash Your Spirit Clean."

Whatever style of music you decide to use at various times during your gatherings, it will carry you to symbolic realms that elude your grasp in any other way. Remember, the music is not an end in itself but a vehicle for the renewal of hearts in worship to God.

✳ Inspirational Readings

Reading is not only for enjoyment and learning; it also is a spiritual practice. The Sacred Scriptures tell us that we are "transformed by the renewing of [our] minds" (Romans 12:2). The key to reading for inspiration is not in the number of books we read but in the way we experience what we do read.

Your circle might choose to read between sessions and then discuss a portion of the book when you are together. Or you might read short passages during the circle gathering for reflection, journaling, and discussion. Here are a few book suggestions to get you started:

But God Remembered: Stories of Women from Creation to the Promised Land, Sandy Eisenberg Sasso. Woodstock, Vermont: Jewish Lights Publishing, 1995. Offers a charming re-embroidery of ancient and modern midrash. ISBN 1879045435.

Heart to Heart Guidebook: A Spiritual Journey for Women and *From the Heart Journal: A Personal Prayer Journal for Women,* Patricia D. Brown. Nashville: Dimensions for Living, 1999. Get your women's spirituality group up and running with these ready-to-use resources. If you like the ideas in this book, you'll love these twelve inspiring gatherings. ISBN 0687070449.

Holy the Firm, Annie Dillard. San Francisco: HarperCollins, 1999. Dillard welcomes you to her little cabin to reflect on the meaning of life. Beautifully written. ISBN 0816165718.

Learning to Lead from Your Spiritual Center, Patricia D. Brown. Nashville: Abingdon Press, 1996. How to keep yourself spiritually centered in the midst of dysfunctional organizations. You'll be relieved to find out, as I did, that you're not crazy— the system is. ISBN 0687006120.

Pilgrim Heart: The Inner Journey Home, Sarah York. San Francisco: Jossey-Bass, 2001. This gentle, practical, and wise book invites you on a spiritual journey. ISBN 0787956953.

Prayer and Our Bodies, Flora Slosson Wuellner. Nashville: Upper Room Books, 1987. Using prayer and guided meditations, Wuellner guides us to greater insight toward our identities as women. All her books are good. ISBN 083805689.

Self and Soul: A Women's Guide to Enhancing Self-Esteem Through Spirituality, Adele Wilcox. New York: Daybreak Books, 1997. This compassionate book teaches women how to make life-changing moves that will take them to new levels of positive self-discovery. Your group will appreciate the exercises at the end of each chapter. ISBN 087596446X.

365 Affirmations for Hopeful Living, Patricia D.

Brown. Nashville: Dimensions for Living, 1992. A year's worth of healing affirmations for groups to use as a daily reader while they are apart. Builds community. ISBN 0687418895.

✳ Other Resources That Give Guidance

This listing of other resources represents only a fraction of what is out there in the arena of women's spirituality. Periodically cruise the shelves of a good women's bookstore, or check out the religious or women's studies sections of your local bookstore as you sip your favorite coffee. Occasionally you'll find something in the self-help category, too. Call or e-mail your friends and ask them what they are using. I call it "sixth sense research," and it is my main way of finding new resources.

Altars Made Easy: A Complete Guide to Creating Your Own Sacred Space, Peg Streep. San Francisco: HarperSanFrancisco, 1997. This book will help release your creativity for your focus center. ISBN 0062514903.

Keep Simple Ceremonies, Diane Eiker and Sapphire, eds. Portland, Maine: Astarte Shell Press, 1995. Contains practical ideas and fully developed examples of prayer rituals you may adapt to use in your gatherings. ISBN 1885349025.

Ritualizing Women: Patterns of Spirituality, Lesley A. Northup. Cleveland, Ohio: Pilgrim Press, 1997. Provides a summary of the current thinking about what is distinctive in women's ritualizing. ISBN 082981213X.

✳ Women's Spirituality Web

There are fascinating spirituality sites to explore on the Internet, but I had to really search for the few attuned to women of the Christian tradition. Changes on the web are daily, so check it out for yourself. There are all sorts of intriguing pages to explore. For starters:

- **www.clas.ufl.edu/users/gthursby/mys/womens.htm** You'll find lots of other links on women's spirituality, women's studies, the Black woman's experience and more.

- **www.faculty.de.gcsu.edu/~dvess/magistra.htm** *Magistra* is a journal of women's spirituality in history. It contains scholarly articles by impressive writers. Go online to read past issues.

- **www.gracecom.org** Link yourself into a circle of inspiration through the labyrinth of Lauren

Artress and the Veriditas staff of Grace Cathedral, San Francisco. The worldwide labyrinth movement offers women a rediscovered way to connect with God through this walking prayer.

- **www.LadySlipper.org** This is a terrific site to check out for music, all recorded by women. Besides having 1,500 titles in their catalog, Lady Slipper is a small independent label whose purpose is to further new musical and artistic directions for women.

- **www.sacredimagination.com** At this women's center for creativity and spirituality, Dana Reynolds invites soulful living through creativity, art and writing in journals.

- **www.spiritworks.org** Talk directly to me about questions you have as you begin your spirituality circle, read an affirmation, order resources, or attend an event where I'm facilitating. Check out the Spiritworks page and send me a message. I'd love to meet you!

- **www.users.csbsju.edu/~eknuth/xpxx/** This page is dedicated to historical sources, book reviews, biographies, and articles that look at faith and feminism.

Finding Our Path

Questa has been blessed. She found a mentor and guide who affirmed her and helped her see the vast possibilities of life. The search causes her to look deeply and find the Christ who gives meaning to the faith that now lives within her. The journey to her heart has been arduous. But now that she has found her path, she sees that she can share it with others, offering the gift of herself living within the heart of God.

—The Quest of the Woman in Search of Her Heart

My hope is that you will find a gathering of women with whom to dream, dance, and delight. I believe that when we dare to become a circle of women, we are more likely to be engaged at the point of our deepest needs, spoken to about the core of our faith, challenged to wrestle with questions and answers, and then to go out as gracious witnesses to our communities. Circles are a woman's place to be formed and transformed.

May you be blessed, like the woman who once again found her heart.

She is driving away with more than she'd come with, and it is almost laughable how pleased she feels . . . and how blessed—and how rich.

—The Quest of the Woman in Search of Her Heart